332.024'2

CHRISTIANS AND MONEY

A Guide to Personal Finance

REV. DONALD W. JOINER — *ANY RELATION TO REV. SUE JOINER, DIAC?*

DISCIPLESHIP RESOURCES
MATERIALS FOR GROWTH IN CHRISTIAN FAITH AND LIFE
P.O. Box 189 • Nashville, TN 37202 • Phone (615) 340-7284

Unless otherwise noted, all scripture quotations are from the New Revised
Standard Version of the Holy Bible, Copyright © 1989 by the Division of
Christian Education of the National Council of the Churches of Christ in the
USA and used by permission.

Library of Congress Card Catalog No. 90-82876

ISBN 0-88177-096-5

DR096B

CONTENTS

PREFACE

I am often asked how I got into the practice of financial planning. Many see it as strange that a pastor is involved in the area of money. I am involved because, as the Apostle Paul said, "I can do no other." God has given me a gift. That gift is to see the relationship of the sacred and the secular in financial planning. To understand the financial planning process and explain it in understandable language is a gift. To join that gift with faith's journey is my invitation to you.

No one ever writes a book alone. I thank God for the gift. I thank Norma Wimberly, Terry Allen, and Tom Rannells for reading the manuscript and giving me help in its formation. I thank Herb Mather for encouraging this journey. The manuscript would have never made it to the editor without Mary Boyd typing it into the computer. Thanks, Mary! The final manuscript would not have been possible without the careful editorial work of Craig Gallaway and Jill Reddig.

Most of all I want to thank my family for understanding when I was writing this book instead of being with them. To them I dedicate this book. To Cathy, who has been my partner in this journey of faith and planning, all I can say is, I love you. To my sons, Paul and Andy, I thank you for the insights you have given me as we have grown together in Christ. May this book invite you further into your journey with God.

INTRODUCTION

There is overwhelming attention given to money in today's world. The number of money-related magazines in bookstores is exceeded only by the number of computer magazines. *USA Today* has an entire section entitled "Money." There is even a cable network dedicated to financial news.

It is almost as if money were coming out of the closet for the first time. Sex, money, politics, and religion were, traditionally, topics never to be brought up in public. The Sixties opened the door to politics and religion. The Seventies and the Eighties brought sex out of the closet. Now it is time for money to become an acceptable topic for discussion. Indeed, it is past time.

Any discussion of money, either what we have or what we do not have, has been discouraged. Many people think the problem with money is that there is more month left at the end of our money. If we just had more money, or less month between pay periods, we could balance our finances.

Bookstores and library shelves are filled with books about money management. Why do we need another book? Isn't there enough written about money and financial planning? Are there not enough financial planners trying to sell us something to solve our money crisis?

There are many good books, financial magazines, television shows, and financial planners ready to help us. Most focus on big incomes and how to make them bigger. They begin with money as the problem and end with money as the solution. The problem is not information. If it were, all we would have to do is read a book or attend one of the many seminars on financial management.

This is not just another book on money management. This is not a book on how to get more money. This is a book about Christians and money. As Christians, we begin not with the mechanics of money management but with our relationship with God. What does that relationship, and our response in faith, have to do with how we manage our money? Jesus said more about money and resources than any other single subject. The object of this book is to help Christians think through the financial planning process in light of their faith.

Christians and Money does offer "how-to" information on financial planning. But more than that, it is an invitation for you to explore the financial planning process in light of your response to God, your personal history, and the world in which you live. Each chapter invites you to explore your feelings and make decisions about your finances—and about your faith. I hope you will be both informed and spiritually formed by what you read here.

The financial planning pyramid shown below will give you an overview of the approach to money management in this book.

FINANCIAL PLANNING PYRAMID

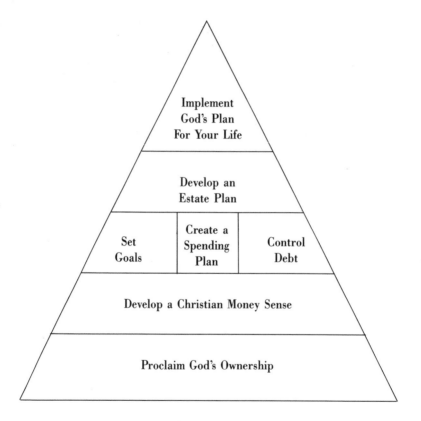

Chapters one and two are foundational to the entire book. They explore faith's perspective on money and basic human patterns of life. Chapter one introduces you to the biblical symbol of the steward as the appropriate measure upon which all resources are managed. Chapter two invites you to examine the dynamics of life which cause you to react to money as you do.

The reason most financial plans fail is because we try to impose strict measures, like a budget, that we eventually abandon. Chapters three and four involve you in designing a spending plan that will work for you. Chapter three begins by asking what you want to accomplish in your financial plan. Then chapter four helps you design a plan to accomplish those objectives.

Since debt is a major problem today, you will look at debt outside the regular planning process. Chapter five explores how debt management can bring spiritual and financial satisfaction. Chapter six reminds us that the stewardship of life does not end at death. Designing an estate plan can be both a financial and spiritual exercise.

Chapter seven brings all these dynamics together into a life plan that you will create. Your life plan will never be completed. It is a journey throughout all of your life. It is always changing. And it is different for each person.

What is the first thing you think of when you hear the words *financial planning?* Most people think of investing in stocks, bonds, and mutual funds. This book is not about investing. It is also not about retirement planning, college planning, tax management, or insurance. Each is an important part of financial planning, but here we start with a more basic foundation.

This book is about you, money, and God. Before you can plan for any of these other areas you must develop a basic spiritual and financial plan. After you have completed the journey in this book, you will be ready to move on to more advanced stages of financial planning.

Assumptions

All of us have assumptions that govern our behavior. We also have assumptions about money. How we earn it, spend it, react to it, and sometimes even avoid it, are directed by our assumptions. The following assumptions are part of my life and faith. They have guided me in writing each chapter of this book.

1. *Christian money management adds an exciting, positive, and affirming dimension to life's plan.*

2. *Our response to money comes from, and touches, the soul.*

3. *The secret of financial planning is in discovering God's purpose and active part in all of life.*

4. *There is a place for tithing in today's financial plan.*

5. *Many people have a feeling of inadequacy in personal money management. Financial planning is assumed to be only for those who have money or for the "experts" in financial planning.*

6. *The financial planning process is available to anyone. Within three months of working with this process, you will be able to see the difference in your financial life.*

7. *Many people are not managing their money. Instead of managing what they have, they are caught up in reacting to the emotions, the sales pitch, or the "wants" of the immediate moment.*

8. *Communication about money (or the lack of communication) causes problems in marriages, families, and personal relationships.*

9. *Excessive debt is an overpowering force and a block to one's faith.*

10. *All debt is not bad. Some debt may be necessary, if it is short-term and includes a planned payoff.*

11. *Charitable giving, now and at death, is an exciting response to the good news of God in Jesus Christ.*

12. *Financial planning involves decisions about what one wants to do about life and faith.*

What assumptions do you hold about management, faith, and values regarding money? Take some time to identify your own assumptions before reading further. Be honest with yourself.

CHAPTER ONE
A FAITHFUL PERSPECTIVE ON MONEY

*We are God's fellow-workers . . . you are God's
building. I am like a skilled master-builder who
by God's grace laid the foundation, and someone
else is putting up the building. Let each take care
how he builds* (1 Corinthians 3:9-11, NEB).

Toni and Jay were struggling for meaning in their life. "We have always
had everything we wanted!" Jay exclaimed to his class. "We never considered
ourselves rich or extravagant. We worked hard to put both of our children
through college. We always lived for them. Now they are gone. Their leaving
has caused us to reevaluate our life. Can the Christian faith help us find
meaning? Can that faith give us hope? Is there any direction in life besides
earning more?"

Cory and Carrie were in the same Sunday school class. They were studying
the story in Luke of the rich farmer who stored everything in his silos. "You
know," Carrie said in response to Jay's question, "we have been struggling
with the same issues. We don't have any children yet. We are getting started.
We are not sure life is meant just to work, earn, and build up our assets. Are
we wrong? As we begin managing our money, does the Christian faith have
any guidance for us?"

Perhaps you share some of the questions these two couples are asking. You
have probably chosen this book because its title links two important areas of
your life, faith and money. By choosing this book, you are proclaiming
yourself a Christian. You may also be saying, "I need help with my finances.
Does the Christian faith have anything to say about financial management?"
The answer is a resounding *yes!*

The terms *money management* and *financial planning* are often used
interchangeably. There really is a difference. Money management is concerned with the earning, managing, saving, and investing of money. Its entire
focus is on the economics of money and what it can do for you.

Financial planning, on the other hand, is an overall examination or
uncovering of one's goals in life, an exploration of one's existing and future
finances, and a plan to coordinate the two. Money management is only one

1

step in financial planning. Christian financial planning is the application of one's Christian faith and values to that financial plan.

Money management focuses on money. The clear goal is to have more at some point in time. The reason for acquiring more money may never be very clear. Societal norms encourage us to earn and accumulate all we can in order to take care of our families and ourselves. We are taught, from an early age, that ultimate security in life rests on how much we can earn and save. That certainly is the norm, isn't it?

Christian financial planning is less interested in how much we have, or even what we do with what we have. It is first a spiritual issue: How much of us does God have? Christian financial planning begins with and focuses on God. The Christian affirms that all we have comes from God. God invites us into a partnership in the ongoingness of creation. It is an invitation, exemplified in Jesus Christ, to claim that intimate relationship with God we call stewardship.

The Steward

Several years ago I was invited to teach the summer session of the seventh grade Sunday school. Part of that summer session was on *stewardship*. I began that Sunday session asking the youth what the word meant. There was complete silence. Silence is not all that unusual when you ask seventh grade students a question. I thought if I tried asking the question in a different way, I would get a response. "How is the word *steward* used today?" I asked. There was again a long silence. Then someone mentioned a steward or stewardess on a plane. I thought, "We're on a roll now." But the listing of their thoughts about the word *steward* stopped. They had never heard the word *steward* or *stewardship* used in their daily life. What does that say about our use of the word?

What are some other words you think of when you hear the word *steward*?

1. Trustee	4. Sharing	7.
2. Custodian	5. Manager	8.
3. Care-giver	6. Caretaker	9.

The word *steward* is not widely used in either ancient times or the modern era. As we grow more concerned about the environment, the word is beginning to be used more often. It is actually used in the Bible only about twenty-six times. There are other terms used, however, with similar meanings. The word *servant* is used in the Old Testament in much the same way as the word *steward*. In the New Testament the word *servant* is also used but with much more familiar meaning, such as "friend" or "trusted companion."

The Greek word for steward is *oikonomos*. It comes from another Greek word, *oikos*, which literally means "residence." The reference is to a

2

structure or building and the close bond which occurs between the inhabitants of the building. The words suggest the intimate responsibility everyone in a residence has for one another. The word *oikonomia* is the word which closely translates to "stewardship." It means the management of the residence. It refers to the task, or often the position, of making sure the residence is managed in such a way that the common good, and the common goal of those who reside within, is accomplished. It is from this word that we get the modern word *economy*.

The English usage of the word *steward* comes from the word *styward*. It literally means "the keeper of animals confined in a pen, corral, or cage." Because such "kept" animals cannot take care of themselves, the "styward" is given the responsibility of their care.

Look in your dictionary to see what it says about the word *steward*. Write your answer in the following space:

A steward is . . .

Name three people who most represent this definition of a steward. Why do you think they represent a steward?

1.

2.

3.

Ownership

A steward is a person who is a manager, a custodian, or a trustee of something owned by someone else. The steward does not own what is managed. It belongs to someone who *trusts* the steward to manage what is being cared for, according to the will and purpose of the real owner.

That's nice, but how does that apply to me and the management of my financial plan? What do I own? What do you own? Would you list your home, an automobile, personal property such as clothes or furniture, a checking account, or maybe even this book? Do you really own these things? Will you own them five years from now or twenty-five years from now? Will you still own them one hundred years from now?

Our culture prides itself on ownership. The work ethic is based on working hard to earn wages, to purchase items which show that we are accomplishing something. Value or meaning in life is linked to what can be purchased. Have you ever patted yourself on the back, as I have, saying with pride, "I deserve this. After all, I have earned it. I have worked hard, and now the right of ownership is mine!" I feel a certain sense of accomplishment in showing off my achievements to others.

With ownership comes the right to do as one pleases with that which is owned. If you own something, you do not need to consult with anyone if you choose to change it, dispose of it, give it away, or even destroy it.

The Christian steward soon discovers and affirms that true ownership is with God. Have you read the first chapter of Genesis and wondered, as I have, about the whole question of creation versus evolution? Did God create this world and everything in it in six days, or did creation evolve over millions of years? We are so caught up in the debate of creation versus evolution that we miss the whole point of the story. The Genesis story is not about *how* the world was begun. It is about *who* created it and, therefore, who owns it.

In the beginning, God created everything from nothing. There was a formless void. There was neither night nor day. There was nothing! From nothing God put together all that we have. What have you ever created out of nothing? Everything I have done has relied on some product, thought, or action of someone or something before me.

Biblical literature is full of references to ownership. God asked Job, "Where were you when I laid the foundations of the earth?" (Job 38:4). Who really did the work? Who, therefore, owns the earth? The psalmist is constantly reminding readers: "The earth is the Lord's and all that is in it" (Psalm 24:1-2); "It is he [God] that made us and we are his" (Psalm 100:3); "The world and all that is in it is mine" (Psalm 50:12). In his instructions to the Israelites, Moses admonishes, "Do not say to yourself, 'My power and the might of my own hand have gotten me this wealth'" (Deut. 8:17).

King David was a powerful man. Both biblical and historical documents

4

point to his success, influence, and power. He was probably the richest person in his time. He spent a vast sum in the construction of the Temple in Jerusalem. He spared no expense. At the dedication of that Temple, all the speeches and accolades pointed to how great David was for this great act. He was given credit for the idea of the Temple, spending his wealth to build it, and encouraging the builders along the way. How swelled my head would be if I were in his shoes! When it came time for him to respond, he did not accept the accolades but pointed to God as the true owner and source of all he had (1 Chron. 29:10-18).

Basil the Great, born in Cappadocia in A.D. 330, states that one truly owns only that which was brought into life from elsewhere. In 1 Timothy 6:7 we are reminded that we brought nothing into this world, and we will take nothing with us when we die. It is the Apostle Paul who asks the searching question: "What do you have that you did not receive? And if you received it, why do you boast as if it were not a gift?" (1 Cor. 4:7).

Remember the four people you met at the beginning of the chapter? At this point in the discussion, Toni is confused: "I don't understand. I've worked hard for what I have. Are you saying God did all the work? Do I get credit for anything I've done?"

One of the greatest tragedies of our contemporary society and the way Christians respond to it is the way we have distorted the whole concept of ownership. The Christian steward begins by affirming the message in Genesis and other books of the Bible that God is the owner of everything. The steward affirms, "All that I have is a gift from God—my thoughts, my health, my family, my singleness, my talents and abilities, even my riches and resources. All that I have comes from God. In the short span of my lifetime, that which I have comes as a trust from God."

Another word closely related to the word *steward* is the word *trustee*. Trustee is a Nordic word used by the Vikings to refer to a person who was left behind when they went out exploring the seas. That person was the most cherished Viking. He was the strongest and most trustworthy of them all. To that person they entrusted not only their wealth and the care of their property but the well-being and safety of their wives and children. This person was given the title "trustee." It was an honor to be selected for this special responsibility. That is the meaning of the word *dominion* in Genesis. It is not a gift of *ownership* but of careful *trusteeship.*

The Christian, as trustee and steward, is in a special relationship with God. We affirm God's ownership and our stewardship. "But I'm confused!" you say. "I want to be a good Christian. I feel that I do own what I have. How can both God and I own what I have? Besides, what difference does it make?"

A better word for what is God's to own and ours to care for may be the word *possession.* God owns; the Christian possesses. Possession is a *right* granted to us by God in the first chapter of Genesis. Possession is not

5

ownership. It may retain qualities of ownership, but it is not ownership. The difference is in the way the Christian perceives that which is possessed. It is a matter of purpose and meaning. The computer on which I am writing this book may have been purchased from my earnings. The technology to design the computer, the components that make up the computer, and the money I used to purchase it all came from God. God owns and allows me to possess. I dedicate it to God. My job is to find out how God wants me to use what I possess.

"I see the difference now," Cory says with an enlightened gleam. "That sure adds meaning to life, doesn't it? What I have is a trust relationship with God. What I possess is not mine but God's. God trusts me to use what is in my possession. That's heavy. There is a lot of responsibility in that thought. Do I really want that responsibility? Do I have a choice?"

The Apostle Paul was right when he asked, "What do you have that you did not receive?" I have a paperweight on my desk that my wife gave me. It is a beautiful burgundy ceramic ball with a gold design running through it. When I see that paperweight and use it on my desk, I think of the generosity and love that were given with that gift. On the other hand, I also have a box that holds my pens and pencils. I bought it so that I would always have something handy with which to write. It is handy all right, but that's all. The paperweight reminds me of my wife's love. I never really think about the pencil box.

The attitude we have concerning ownership will make a significant difference in how we accomplish our financial plan. That's what Jesus meant when he said, "Where your treasure is, there your heart will be also" (Luke 12:34). Where is your heart concerning what you possess? Do you own these things or do they own you?

Cars have always been my downfall. I like to keep them clean and as new as the day I brought them home from the dealership. I take pride in how they look. I would get angry if someone hit my car with a car door or scratched it while walking by. I often wondered how I would react if I had an accident. Then one day our son called to say he had had an accident with our new car. The car was one we had wanted and saved for. It was only two months old. How did I react? I was surprised. Ownership was suddenly less important than my son's health and well-being. The Christian steward possesses but is not possessed by what he or she has.

How would you describe what you possess? What do you have that could be characterized as owning you? What would happen if someone took it away?

6

Acknowledging God's ownership is an important step in Christian financial planning. To acknowledge God's ownership, find a place to let God, in nature, speak to you. You might want to take a leisurely walk, sit in a boat in the middle of a lake, or sit quietly in a favorite park or forest. Write down your thoughts, concerns, and struggles about God's ownership.

The Christian steward is a grateful receiver. What are some of the things you can list for which you are grateful?

The words *grateful* and *gratitude* are signs of a faithful stewardship. Say or sing the Doxology, which acknowledges with gratitude God's part in our life:

> Praise God from whom all blessings flow;
> Praise God all creatures here below;
> Praise God above ye heavenly host;
> Praise Father, Son, and Holy Ghost. Amen.

Praise God with the psalmist as you read at least three of these psalms: Psalm 8, Psalm 23, Psalm 24, Psalm 47, Psalm 50, Psalm 84, Psalm 100, Psalm 148, Psalm 150.

Partnership

As Christian stewards, we recognize everything we have as a gift of God. As a gift, we receive each possession differently than if we owned it and simply used it for our own purposes. As a steward, we receive what we have in relation to God's purpose in all of life.

In 1876 Thomas Huxley visited America especially to speak at the consecration of the new Johns Hopkins University. Prior to this stop at Johns Hopkins, he toured the United States. In his message to the university following this tour, he reflected on the grandeur of this new country: "I cannot say that I am in the slightest degree impressed by your bigness or your material resources. Size is not grandeur; territory does not make a nation. The great issue about which hangs the terror of overhanging fate is, 'What are you going to do with all these things?'"

As Christian stewards we recognize that we may have organized the world, subjected it to our control, industrialized it, automated it, politicized it, and polluted it—but God still owns it. All that we have is a gift from God. All that we do with it is our gift *to* God. We miss the point, however, if all we focus on is the act of possession. Thomas Huxley was right: All we have is nothing, until we decide what we are going to do with what we have.

True meaning and purpose in life are revealed to us when we discover how God intends us to use that which we possess. The Christian steward discovers meaning and purpose in life in relation to God's call in Jesus Christ. John reminds us that God sent Jesus that we might have life in all of its abundance. That is not a call to accumulation but a call to fulfillment under Christ. Paul reveals the meaning of that call when he says we are called to be co-creators, co-workers, or partners with God in the ongoingness of creation (1 Cor. 3:9). The purpose of our possessing is in direct response to our prayer for God's kingdom to come "on earth as it is in heaven."

The relation of the steward to his or her possessions and to God's purpose for the steward lies within the meaning of the word *partner*. A partnership is an agreement by two or more persons to engage in some common activity. That activity may be a team sport, a marriage, or a business adventure. Ideally, each member of the partnership is always acting not only for him or herself but for the partner as well. That partnership is based upon a common purpose and an intimate relationship that allows one partner to trust the other partner with accomplishing their common goal.

The story of Joseph in Genesis is a story about a man in partnership with another. You remember the story of Joseph, don't you? Most of the time we think of Joseph as the story of jealous brothers. We picture Joseph in a pit, his brothers standing over it with the coat of many colors. That is where we usually stop with Joseph. But now, as Paul Harvey says, "for the rest of the story."

8

Joseph came out of the pit and eventually was made the second most powerful person in Egypt. Only the Pharaoh was more powerful. The Pharaoh held the position of owner. Joseph made the decisions about the management of all of Pharaoh's riches and power. Joseph lived an exemplary life of comfort and influence. Joseph owned nothing. It all belonged to Pharaoh.

Joseph knew the Pharaoh so well that he could decide what needed to be done without ever consulting the Pharaoh. But even more intimate than the relationship with Pharaoh was Joseph's relationship with God. Joseph had his good times and his bad times in Egypt. He lived beyond the circumstances of the moment, because he saw that God had a plan. When Joseph was successful, however, he did not take the credit. "It was not me but God through me" was Joseph's motto. What he did, he did because he saw his part in *God's* plan.

Being a partner with God means developing a relationship with God that is so intimate that we know what God wants us to do. When I was a child, my mother sometimes said, "Is that what Jesus would want you to be doing?" That question has remained with me as a question about all my actions, including my finances. When God and I are partners, God becomes the CEO and I become the managing partner. I turn to God for advice as we go on together. As partners, God's business is my business, and my business is God's business.

Jesus told a parable of an astute businessman who was going on a long business trip. He was a success. He had a large group of persons working for him. On this particular trip he was going to be out of range of communications. (This was before the introduction of the cellular phone.) He called his three most trusted employees to meet with him. "I'm going to be away from my business for awhile. You three vice-presidents have shown exceptional skill in understanding how I run the business. You understand me. I trust that my business will be run by you in the same manner I would run it if I were here. I'll see you when I return."

To each of his trusted vice-presidents he gave a specific responsibility. To Mei was given the responsibility of manufacturing. To Brent was given the responsibility of sales and marketing. To Penny was given the responsibility as financial officer. Each was given a specific task.

This is a familiar story. You can read about it in Matthew 25:14-30 and draw your own conclusions. This story explores many issues. For our purposes here, it is an illustration of our relationship with God. God is the owner. God is not an absentee owner, however, but one very much involved in the ongoing work of the kingdom. Each of us is given a part in the running of God's business. God owns the world, and we are honored to be given a position of importance in running God's world.

That is both challenging and scary, isn't it? It is exciting to me to discover that God's trust in me is so complete that I am invited to be a full partner. In that trust, I want to accept the rich challenge of conducting God's business. Yet I know how untrustworthy I can be at times. I also know that whenever I try to do something without my partner, I fail. That's true for me in all of life, including my financial planning.

The story Jesus told of the rich farmer (Luke 12:16-20) was not a condemnation of his wealth but showed that he had lost sight of his purpose as a partner. Seeing how well he had done, the farmer praised his own accomplishments. His only concern was to build bigger barns to store those accomplishments. His sin was not in his success or even in his accumulation. His sin was in losing sight of the true ownership of his crops. He believed he was completely responsible for his own wealth and failed to realize that his only security was with God.

One way of knowing what God proposes for us in the partnership is in what "gifts" we have. *Gifts* is a theological term roughly associated with talents. *Talents* are those areas of expertise that we have developed and use. Isiah Thomas, of the Detroit Pistons, has a talent as a basketball player. Following the Detroit Pistons' win as world champions, Thomas was named most valuable player of the series. Others have exciting talents as singers, as actors, or as politicians. Talents are those "skills" we have developed. They are usually used for personal gain, employment, or hobbies.

The Apostle Paul talks about gifts in Romans 12, 1 Corinthians 12, and Ephesians 4. He uses the analogy of the body to describe the function of gifts. The body is many parts: the ear, nose, feet, tongue, heart. Each part has a separate function. But the body can be the body only if all the parts work together for the common good. "Gifts" may look like talents. They are called "gifts" because they come from God, to be used to accomplish God's purposes for life.

By training, I am an ordained minister, called to help the world and all those within it to experience the good news of God in Jesus Christ. I enjoy the relationship of pastor to a local congregation. One gift I have, however, is understanding money and how it works. Because God has given me that gift, I am expected, as part of my contribution to the partnership, to use that gift to help others.

God provides all that we have—whether gifts, talents, money, or possessions. God gives us what we have to use in accomplishing God's kingdom. Turning now to several specific areas of stewardship, how will you respond to God's call in your life?

Examples

　　1. I will tithe ($_____ of my income, per month) for God's work in my local congregation and the world.

10

2. I will evaluate my accumulation in relationship to my calling as a steward. With my excess I will:

   A. Give to the local thrift shop.

   B.

   C.

3. I will pledge a tithe of my time to the following in God's name:

4. I will work actively for environmental concerns by: Recycling newspapers, cans, and bottles. I will plant ten new trees.

5.

6.

7.

8.

How do you represent your partner:

   In your receiving?

   In your giving?

   In your ownership?

In your spending?

In your use of time?

In your family/singleness?

How will the concept of partnership with God make a difference in your financial planning? How we view God, how we see who we are and what we have as Christians in relationship with God, will influence how successful our Christian financial plan will be. Seeing God as owner of all we possess places a different perspective on what we have. Responding to God's call to be a partner places importance and meaning on what we do. The key word in the understanding of who we are with God is the word *steward*.

The distinction between secular and sacred, between what we own and what is God's, disappears as we see ourselves as Christian stewards. There is no question about whether or not we are stewards. The issue is always what kind of stewards we are. The issue is not money. The issue of your stewardship has very little to do with how much you earn or how much you give. It all boils down to, "How much of *you* does God have?"

The steward begins affirming God's ownership. The steward accepts God's invitation to partnership. The steward celebrates life as a gift of adventure.

12

CHAPTER TWO
DEVELOPING A CHRISTIAN MONEY SENSE

> *Therefore I tell you, do not worry about your*
> *life, what you will eat, or about your body, what*
> *you will wear. For life is more than food, and the*
> *body more than clothing. Consider the ravens:*
> *they neither sow nor reap, they have neither*
> *storehouse nor barn, and yet God feeds them. Of*
> *how much more value are you than the birds!*
> *And can any of you by worrying add a single*
> *hour to your span of life? (Luke 12:22-25).*

Financial planning, for many, is a collection of data, the establishment of forms, cash flow projections, and statements of net worth. Yet the finest financial plan is worthless until you uncover your money sense. The most elaborate plans, the most detailed examination of your financial statement, is useless until you discover why you respond to money the way you do.

Financial planners are often called into the picture as a last resort. Crisis has taken over all money management. Whatever is tried, fails. People look confused when I sit down with them and ask questions about their personal life. They want to fix the problem of "more month left at the end of their money." They cannot understand why I ask questions about their childhood and about their parents. They soon discover that they have a lot of hidden feelings, experiences, fears, and anxieties about money that affect the way they face or avoid money issues. Until you discover your money sense, you may well be doomed to financial bondage and failure.

Dwight and Joan were exceptionally fine people. I knew them through the church. They came to me because they were in a severe financial and spiritual bind. They had been active church members. But now they were avoiding their church friends and staying away from church. Money was so tight that they could not pay their tithe. Feeling guilty about their giving, they just stayed away.

They wanted a plan, almost as a last resort to avoid personal bankruptcy. They needed to get out of the deep financial hole they were in. I listened to them talk, then I asked about their childhood. Dwight was raised in a family

13

that had very little. As a child he saw what others had and wanted what his family could not afford. At age nine he started a paper route after school. Everything came hard for him. Joan, however, came from a far different situation. She had everything she wanted. Her parents, though not wealthy by any means, always had money to do what they wanted. When Joan wanted something, she went out and got it.

Ten years before Dwight and Joan came to me, Joan's parents died within six months of each other. Joan was an only child. All her parents had saved over the years went to Joan. For ten years Dwight and Joan lived what they thought was an exciting life. They took trips, sent the kids to every camp, outing, or school excursion they wanted. They had no plans for the money. They both worked, except for one year Dwight took off to "discover himself" six years ago. They relied on the money from her parents' estate and built a lifestyle around it. Then it happened. The money was gone. Some inappropriate investments and a large tax bill for previous years caught up with them.

They continued to live a lifestyle of comfort and ease. But there was no extra money, except what they earned. By the time they came to me, they had used up their home equity line of credit and had over $13,000 charged on nine credit cards. Joan explained that her father had worked a lifetime to leave them an inheritance that they spent in a short time. The money seemed to have a personality of its own, directing them in all they did. That "personality" was their money sense.

Each of us has a money sense that directs how we respond to money issues in our life. That money sense shapes how we earn a living, how we spend our earnings, and how we react to others as they earn, manage, and spend. Few of us are aware of our personal money sense. But it directs and influences, both positively and negatively, how we respond to, or avoid, money issues that confront us daily.

Every person's money sense is unique to that person's life experience. No two people, even those born to the same parents, have the same money sense. No two people, even those married to each other for years, will have the same money sense. Until you uncover your personal money sense, you will be unable to understand why you act as you do around financial issues.

It is like three blind men describing an elephant. The first man climbs a ladder. Feeling the side of the elephant, he describes it as a big barn. The second man touches the feet of the elephant and feels the coarse hair. He describes the elephant as a large porcupine. The third man feels the trunk and exclaims that the elephant is nothing more than a large snake. For as much as each of these men experienced, they were right. But someone needs to experience the whole animal to get the correct perspective on an elephant.

So it is with our money sense and our financial plan. There are many parts which make up the whole. When we unpack our money sense we will soon discover why we respond the way we do to financial issues. Factors that

14

have touched and formed your money sense include, but are not limited to: childhood experiences with money, how your parents responded (or avoided) money issues; economic, social, and cultural experiences with money; experiences with money during your adult life; and how you see what you have in relation to God and God's purposes for life.

Factors Affecting Our Money Sense

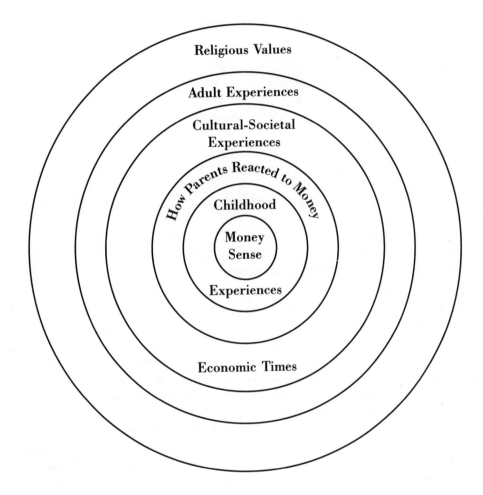

Response to financial issues, conscious or not, is just as important as the actual financial plan. Behavior shapes attitudes as much as attitudes shape behavior. Until you come to grips with the factors making up your money sense, all the plans in the world will not work.

Before we continue any further, consider these questions:

Do you see money as the paper, or coinage, on which is printed the currency of exchange? Or do you see what money can do for you?

Do you see money as a storehouse of value? Or do you see money as a necessary evil in this world?

Do you see money as a means to an end, a necessary item to accomplish your goals? Or is money the goal?

How would you define money? Write three or four sentences here.

Money does not have any value in and of itself. It is only worth the value someone gives to it. That value may change overnight. A missionary told me recently of her experience in Brazil. Overnight the Brazilian currency was worth half of what it was the day before. Even as I write this, East and West Germany have changed over to one currency. One week there was a one-to-one exchange of the deutsche mark and the Ostmark. The next week the Ostmark was worth only half a deutsche mark.

Money only has the value that one gives it. For some, money represents power and security. For some, money promises happiness. Others see money as a problem capable of producing misery. For some, the value of money resides in what it can purchase. For others the accumulation of money is an end in itself. For still others, money represents the possibility of undertaking philanthropic activities. Describe some of the values you give to money.

1.

2.

16

3.

4.

5.

Childhood Experiences

Robert Fulghum, in his popular book *All I Really Need to Know I Learned in Kindergarten*, has expressed an important principle in financial planning. His thesis states that all we really need to get along in life, how to treat people, the manners that govern either our conscious or subconscious behavior, became part of us in our early childhood. So it is with our financial plan. That which causes us to respond to money issues, whether we are a spender or a saver, a miserly stooge or an extravagant spendthrift, whether we are prone to high debt or pay cash before we purchase an item, may well have been determined, maybe not in kindergarten, but certainly by the time we began our teens.

Hidden values from childhood usually impact our behavior without any conscious forethought. Have you, as I have, out of frustration, anger, or sheer exhaustion, shouted at your children, spouse, friend, or even the dog? When the words came out, or later when you settled down, did you think, "Wait a minute, I don't really believe that. Where did that come from?" Sayings by our parents and teachers, as well as our own experiences with money as children, direct how we respond to money issues today. Those sayings and experiences float around somewhere in our subconscious. Some become verbal statements, others just annoying habits. Those habits learned as a child will direct how you respond to money until you come to identify and name them, evaluate their appropriateness to who you are today, and then decide to either formally adapt them to your money sense, or bid them leave.

I enjoy opportunities to be with my brother or sister. It is especially fun when we begin recalling times from our childhood. It is like going through a box of old snapshots. Moments I had forgotten are brought back to my consciousness. Let's have a family reunion with childhood experiences around money. What do you remember from your childhood? By the way, memories may not always be accurate. But they are your memories. Whether fact or fiction, it is your perception of those memories (like the blind men and the elephant) that will direct your money sense.

Several years ago I had the pleasure of being part of a group thinking about money in our lives. It was a weekend experience organized by a group called Ministry of Money, out of Gaithersburg, Maryland. It was an exciting time of getting in touch with myself. Part of the preparation for that event

17

was to write a "money autobiography." I found it helpful to recall those perceptions I had of my childhood growing up in Detroit. I was born just prior to the end of World War II. My family never had much, but I never felt I was deprived of anything. The most important thing I remember about money as a child was that if I wanted something, I had to save for it.

I remember having an allowance. It wasn't much. But with that allowance, I had to buy my own candy down at the penny candy store (shows my age, doesn't it) or an ice cream cone at Brown's Creamery on Yacama. At about age eight, I began selling Christmas cards and wrapping paper door-to-door. This gave me enough money to buy presents.

What I really wanted was a paper route. But the secondhand bike I had was not sturdy enough to hold all those papers. So I sold magazine subscriptions door-to-door and delivered the neighborhood newspaper on Wednesdays, until I had enough to buy that new bike. How proud I was to be able to deliver papers on my own route. I discovered the value of money to accomplish goals.

I always had money in my pocket. But I hardly ever spent it. My spending was future-oriented. I remember my experience as an eleven-year-old with cigarettes. I tried them like everyone else around me. Then one day all I could see was how much money I was burning up. So I quit.

Having money available to accomplish my plans was important, whether buying a bike or saving for college. That explains a lot about me now. I can carry money in my pocket or keep it in the bank without feeling it call to me, "Spend me, spend me!" Sometimes that becomes an obsession. I "need" to have an account with money in it. I may not know what it's for. I need to have a balance there in case it is needed. When that balance is low, and sometimes that is more often than I like, I get anxious. Then I go back to Luke 12 and read Jesus' warning once more.

I worked all through high school, college, and graduate school. I worked not because my parents made me but because I liked the feeling of having money. I always had a balance in my savings account. I hated being in debt. I sometimes think I missed a lot of activities and friendships because I worked so much. But when I wanted to go to college, the money was there.

Three ideas have directed my money sense. First, if I want something, I must work and save for it. Second, if I want something, I must rely on myself to get it. Those may not be bad ideas, as such. But they conflict with the third idea directing my money sense—that God is the provider and I am the steward. I have been working to bring the first two ideas into harmony with the third in my money sense. I am not there yet. But I have come a long way.

18

What about you? What experiences with money do you recall from your childhood? Write down both good and awkward moments you had as a child.

Did you get an allowance? When did you first get an allowance? How much was it? What did you do with the money you received as an allowance or as a gift?

When did you first work to earn money? Describe why you went to work, what you did for a job, what you did with the money, and how you felt.

Parents' Attitude

Your parents' attitude toward money, how they responded to financial situations when you were growing up, also affects how you respond to similar situations today. Some of the ways your parents responded to financial decisions were much the same way their parents responded, and their parents, down the cycle of generations.

How your parents reacted to financial situations was their way of dealing with, or avoiding, the situations of their day. Little did they know how foundational their actions would be to your money sense. What they did may not have been wrong. Your money sense is the result of many persons and events. How your parents responded is just one influence on your money sense.

Can you recall how your parents reacted to money when you were a child? Sometimes I get caught up in my parents' influence at the most inopportune times. I remember when my two sons were eight and six years old. It seems they were always asking for something. I don't remember what they were asking for in this particular situation, but I remember my response was, "We cannot do that; there's no money." Later that same day my wife and I decided that the whole family would go out to eat. My oldest son said, "Dad, I thought you said we didn't have any money." He was right. I was giving him mixed signals. Instead of explaining the situation, I responded much the same way my parents responded when I was a child. The difference was that my

son was secure enough to ask me about it. The amount of money we h
not the issue. How we had decided to spend it was the issue.

Carlos and Maria were having trouble with their financial plan. Like many
others, they got to the point of not being able to pay their bills. They had a
budget that Maria kept, but it never seemed to work. In discussing their
parents' attitudes about money, Maria reluctantly shared a "game" her
mother played with her father. Her mother would tell her father something
cost a lot less than it really did, just to keep him happy. In fact, whenever
Maria's dad would say no to something Maria wanted, her mother gave her
the money anyway. Her father never knew. Maria thought that was the way it
was supposed to be. The budget didn't work because Maria was hiding the
true costs of running the house. That was what she had learned from her
parents.

What memories can you recall about how your parents responded to money
issues when you were a child?

What were the messages about money that your parents left with you?

Describe an occasion when you and your parents discussed money or had an argument involving money.

Was there a time when you were a child that your family experienced a financial crisis? Describe that event. How did you feel? How did your parents react?

If you have brothers and sisters, find a time to talk to them about their childhood recollections about money. What do they recall?

What messages are you giving, or have you given, your children about money?

Economic, Social, and Cultural Experiences

The economic climate, the social setting, and our Western culture all affect the way we respond to financial issues out of our money sense. Money talk may well find its way into our life in the Nineties. In the past, sex and money were forbidden topics of discussion except in intimate conversations, and even then we would avoid any discussion if at all possible. Then sex talk came into vogue in the 1980s with Dr. Ruth and Joyce Brothers. Yet money is still taboo. We can talk about the national economy, the price of milk, or the local school budget—but we are still uncomfortable discussing *our own* money.

Gene and Violet have two daughters, now both grown and with families of their own. When the girls were growing up, their parents never discussed money with them. Whenever the girls wanted something, they just asked for it. Gene was the sole breadwinner of the family.

Gene still makes all the important financial decisions. He gives Violet whatever she needs to pay the bills. He takes care of the rest. He believes that his wife can do the shopping, but Gene always balances the checkbook himself. "After all, women don't really understand money," is how he puts it.

They never talk about money. Violet doesn't know how much insurance they have, or with whom for that matter. She knows there is a safe-deposit box at the bank, but Gene has the key. She doesn't even know what is in it. Should Gene die or become seriously ill, Violet would be in a difficult situation. Since the two daughters are not aware of their parents' financial situation, when their parents die, the two women have to settle their estate without any of the critical information they need.

Unfortunately this story of Gene and Violet is all too common in our culture. I have never understood why society has assumed money management is a male-oriented talent. Traditional attitudes toward money and women have been painfully slow to change. Many people in our society, men and women alike, still believe that handling money is a man's job. Yet there is no basis in fact to that belief. For example, until a few years ago, the chief financial officer of Apple Computers, at a time of rapid growth for the company, was a woman.

Money management and financial planning are not gender sensitive. Each person must examine his or her own ability to manage a financial plan. If both husband and wife are able, share the responsibility. If no one is able, then seek outside assistance. But whoever is charged with the responsibility, all members of the family should be kept aware of the situation and made part of all major decisions.

24

What factors in society affect your money sense?

Bumper stickers often reflect the societal norms that govern us. Two that I have seen include: "I'm spending my children's inheritance" and "The one who dies with the most toys wins." Make a list of bumper stickers or slogans you have seen, and explain what they say about society's contribution to your money sense.

Our society has passed down sayings from generation to generation. These sayings about money are our culture's way of teaching us money sense. I have listed several sayings. What other sayings can you remember?

"A penny saved is a penny earned."
"Where your treasure is there your heart will be also."
"Time is money."
"Waste not, want not."
"The buck stops here."

How you handle or avoid money may well be in response to where you were born and economic conditions in your family when you were a child. Jon is clear that his dad's sudden unemployment and extended time without a job when Jon was eight have a strong impact on how he sees money today. Insurance and emergency savings are important to Jon, even if he must give up other things he wants. He will not get in the same situation his father was in.

Jerry likes to compare himself to his two sisters. He sees a large difference in the way they approach money issues and how he approaches money. His two sisters were born in the early Twenties. By the time of the Depression, following the stock market disaster of 1929, they were very much aware of the lack of money. Jerry, however, was born in 1931. A child of the Depression, he remembers stories by his parents and sisters, but he did not experience the economic impact as did his sisters.

Jerry's sisters live even today under the belief that another depression will hit them. They pay cash for everything. They will owe no one. They have large amounts of money in bank certificates of deposit (never in stocks), money hidden in their mattresses, and canned goods stored in the pantry. They live each day as if the depression were right around the corner. When it happens, they will be ready.

Lynette and her brother, on the other hand, were born immediately after World War II. They experienced a far different economic situation. They were part of a boom. What their parents lacked when they were growing up, they were bound and determined to let their children have. Every new toy, every new fashion was to be theirs. Unfortunately, now that Lynette and her brother are adults, they want to live the same way they did in their childhood. They have no sense of savings; after all, they will earn more next year. So the new Nikes for their kids, the new BMW, even the Formula One speedboat, are not too much.

26

The economic conditions during our childhood affect our money sense today as much as the current economic conditions. What is your economic money sense? Do you want to get it under your control, rather than you under its control? Explain the economic times for the nation, and your family, from the time you were five until you graduated from high school. How have these economic conditions affected your money sense?

Adult Experiences

Focusing on issues of our childhood and how they touch our money sense is not to say that our current economic experiences do not affect us. What happens in the economy, as well as what happens in our personal life, touches our money sense.

Felicia's husband died, leaving her with three small children, no insurance, and a lot of bills to pay. Maurice's wife filed for divorce and left him with very little. When Felicia and Maurice became friends, each approached their new relationship with a sense of distrust. Their money sense was bruised by their adult experience.

Whenever we encounter new, intimate relationships, we discover new attitudes, experiences, and expectations about money. We can either confront them or ignore them and face the consequences. Marriage changes the entire dynamic of your money sense. Books on marriage and the family, pastors, marriage and family counselors, and even page one of USA Today declare that most divorces have at the core of their problem some money issue. Couples, whether married or significant others, avoid discussing money as if it were the plague.

27

Kathy and Bob were lucky. Early in their marriage they discovered they had a problem. Kathy was treated by her parents like most girls growing up in the Fifties. When she wanted something, she simply asked for $5.00 or whatever she needed, and her parents gave it to her. She had very little concept of the value of money. She did what she wanted, got what she wanted, and there was no real sense that money was limited. Bob, on the other hand, had to work his way through high school and college. He seemed to have more than some of his friends, but he was always working.

Soon after they married, the first money crisis interrupted their happy marriage. Bob was the financial manager. Both he and Kathy had good jobs, but Bob paid the bills. It seemed that the credit card balances were getting higher each month. Bob never said anything to Kathy. She kept buying what she wanted, and Bob kept quiet about the bills he couldn't pay. Bob became angry and withdrawn. Kathy didn't know what to think. She thought he was having an affair. They never talked about their feelings. It wasn't until they went to see their pastor that the problem came into focus.

Couples must discover their individual money sense early in their marriage. By discussing their history, experiences, and money sense they will know how to respond to money issues as they face them. A new money sense can then be developed which can influence how they manage their financial plan in the future.

How would you describe your spouse's (or significant other's) money sense?

28

After you and your spouse have each discovered your money sense, compare your stories. How does your money sense complement your spouse's money sense?

Together with your spouse, significant other, or close friend, discuss what you would do in the following situations:

1. You win $10,000 from the state lottery. What will you do?

2. Your company is being taken over by a larger corporation. The new corporation will start a new pension plan. Your old pension will pay you $50,000. What will you do with it?

3. You are in a car accident. You will be out of work for a year. Social Security and disability insurance will not begin for another three months. What will you do?

4. Your favorite aunt died last week. Her estate is finally being settled and you will inherit $1,000,000. What will you do?

5. Draw a straight line. On the far left of the line, write "The Worst of Times." On the far right, write "The Best of Times." Where are you now on that spectrum of your financial life? Why did you place yourself in that position?

6. Let your memory wander back to a time when you felt happiest and most comfortable in your life. It may be a time when you had very little money but made the most of it. Describe that situation, and tell why it was such a good time for you.

Religious Values

The religious values we hold affect our money sense in various ways. Chapter one holds before us the role of the steward as the model for Christians and money. The Christian steward declares God to be the owner of all he or she possesses. Our relationship to what we have is as a partner with God. But it is not what we have, not only what we do with what we have, or even how we manage what we have that is of key importance. What is important is our relationship with God.

Sometimes we misinterpret biblical guidance about money. Myths about faith and money often guide our money sense into conflict with reality. Three of those myths are ones I have heard stated in religious circles across the continent and across denominations.

First, *wealth is sinful and wrong.* I hear this in many ways from different churches. But then there is an ironic conflict. In the same breath that we are told not to have money, the church then turns around and asks us to increase our giving. It doesn't really make sense to me. Jesus was never against wealth as such. He often chose wealthy people as friends and companions. He chose to go to the home of Zacchaeus, a wealthy man. He stayed at the large home of friends in Bethany. Wasn't it there that Mary brought expensive oil, which cost as much as a month's normal wage, to anoint Jesus' feet? His close friend and follower, Joseph of Arimathea, gave his own tomb, a sure sign of wealth even today, to place Jesus' body when it was taken from the cross.

Jesus was not against wealth. What Jesus was against was anything that separates us from the love of God. Money often does just that. If money becomes the all-consuming goal for anyone, then that person has been separated from God. But it can also become a powerful tool if we see what we have in the true perspective of God's will.

Second, *poverty is next to godliness.* It's funny—I have never heard this from someone living in a cardboard house. This myth is usually held by those of us who have more. But there is nothing more godly about poverty than there is sinful about wealth. In fact, in Proverbs 30:8, Solomon prays to God to give him neither poverty nor wealth. There can be problems with either. For some the vow of poverty, to live in a monastic community, may be appropriate. All of us must *put our lifestyle in perspective with our faith.* The vow of poverty is the answer for some, but certainly not for everyone. Simplicity may well be the call for today. Richard Foster has written an exciting book on *The Freedom of Simplicity.* We may not need to sell all we possess, but we certainly may need the freedom of a less complex lifestyle.

Third, *money is the root of all evil.* Myth three is probably the most misquoted and misunderstood statement about money we hear. The quote from 1 Timothy 6:10 is part of Paul's letter to his young friend. In that letter he is warning Timothy about false teachings and the lure of temptations. But Paul never said money in and of itself was evil or corrupt. *There is nothing inherently evil in money.* What Paul wrote Timothy about was that "the *love* of money is the root of all evil." This is the same thing Jesus said over and over again. Gain the right perspective about money, know what it can do with your help to accomplish God's will, and then dedicate it to God.

Can you name other myths and sayings that guide your money sense?

The relationship we have with God is the most important factor in all of our Christian life. Jesus Christ, as Lord of life and all we possess, came to show us life, that we might have it in its freedom and its abundance. When we see money as a tool to accomplish God's will and purpose in life, as revealed in Jesus Christ, money becomes a blessing rather than a curse in our lives.

Are you ready to dedicate what you have to God's will and purpose?

1. Take out any denomination of paper money.
2. Center your thoughts on the words printed on that currency, "In God We Trust."
3. This denomination of currency does not represent a commodity of secular exchange; it represents people. Look at it carefully. Picture the many faces of those who have had this money in their possession. Think of the hard work and sacrifice this currency represents. Think of the love that has been expressed because of this currency. Did someone buy flowers for a close friend? Did this currency purchase tickets for some special event? Think of the good causes it has gone to support.
4. Contemplate other places, events, and people, where this currency has been.
5. Think of the good that might yet come from this currency.
6. First, read the following prayer. Then *pray* the prayer.

Lord, see this bill! It frightens me.
You know its secrets, you know its history.
How heavy it is!
It scares me, for it cannot speak.
It will never tell all it hides in its creases.
It will never reveal all the struggles and efforts it represents, all the
    disillusionment and slighted dignity.
It is stained with sweat and blood.
It is laiden with all the weight of the human toil which makes its worth.

O Lord, I offer you this bill with its joyous mysteries, its sorrowful
    mysteries.
I thank you for all the life and joy it has given.
I ask your forgiveness for the harm it has done.
But above all, Lord, I offer it to You as a symbol of all the labors
    of men, indestructible money,
Which tomorrow will be changed into your eternal life.

—From *Prayers* by Michael Quiost

Used with permission of Sheed & Ward, Kansas City, MO.

Write down your feelings about this dedication.

~ ~

CHAPTER THREE

MANAGING FOR FINANCIAL FREEDOM

Be careful then how you live, not as unwise
people but as wise, making the most of the
time. . . . So do not be foolish, but understand
what the will of the Lord is (Ephesians 5:15-17).

Failure to plan is planning to fail.

Anonymous

Money talks,
I don't deny.
I heard it once.
It said, good-bye.

Anonymous

When I look back, some of the best times were those times when we had very little. Knowing that we didn't have much caused us to watch our pennies more. We were more creative then in our entertainment and in our spending. We had to make each dollar count. We didn't have much. There wasn't much we wanted either. Wanting only made things worse. We didn't have the money. We wouldn't have the money next week either—or next month or the next month. Since we knew that, it made it a lots easier to live. Why have things changed? We make so much more money now. But where is it? And where is the fun?

Most of us have had a similar time in life. There were only limited finances to go around. But we accepted it. Pete and Jan were like that. They were married during Jan's third year of college. Pete had already graduated and had a job in the small college town where Jan went to school. He didn't earn much, but it was enough to get them through Jan's last two years of school. When Jan graduated, they both got jobs in the same area.

From just $14,500 a year they were now making nearly $35,000. They felt they were "millionaires." They had gone without for so long, they could now

35

have all they wanted. It was as if a dam broke in their money sense. For graduation Pete bought Jan that new red Volkswagen convertible she had always wanted. After they moved, Pete traded in his old Ford Escort and bought a year-old, but practically new, Corvette. They had good jobs now and the sixty months of payments on Jan's car and the forty-eight months on Pete's car would be paid in no time.

They rented a large apartment located halfway between their jobs. The apartment they had in college was furnished. They went out and bought new furniture, a big-screen television, VCR, stereo, and a fabulous new waterbed. They met new friends and went out to eat two or three times a week. Soon they went on a trip to Cancun with a group from Jan's office. Life was great! But then something happened. About seven months after Jan's graduation, they found themselves in a bind. After paying all their bills, and even then Jan only paid the minimum on the charge accounts, there was no money left. The refrigerator was bare. There was no gas in either car, and the car insurance was now due on Jan's VW. What happened? They were making so much money. Where had it gone?

Jan and Pete saw their problem earlier than most couples and sought help. It is a common scenario. Having gone without for so long, the new source of income set free all the pent-up urges to buy the things they wanted. They were now earning $2,275 a month after taxes and had committed themselves to:

Monthly Payments	
$ 363.00	Jan's car
399.00	Pete's car
599.00	Furniture
550.00	Rent
157.00	Utilities
169.00	Credit card (vacation)
90.00	Credit card (minimum payments)
$2,327.00	

Out-of-control spending is the cause of most money problems. This is true whether you earn $10,000 a year, $35,000 like Jan and Pete, or $1 million a year. Without some spending plan, without a comprehensive understanding of your income and expenses, you will always find yourself in trouble, no matter how much you earn.

A financial plan coordinates your assets (what you own), your liabilities (what you owe), your income, and your expenses in order to achieve your goals and dreams. The premise of a financial plan is: If you know what you have and where it is going, you have an excellent chance of controlling it, rather than it controlling you.

A plan is intentional. It is not simply a New Year's Eve resolution to spend less but a well-thought-out, written design to accomplish specific goals. It may be a complicated, computer-generated, fifty-page report from your local financial planner or a one-page plan on what you will do, by when, and how. In a few pages you will find step-by-step instructions for creating *your* distinctive plan.

Every financial plan is unique. It is designed for specific needs and a particular lifestyle. What is working for your friends may not be right for you.

A financial plan is a process. It is never a fixed plan. It is always changing. It changes as you change. It changes as your income changes. It changes as your lifestyle changes, whether that change is marriage, birth of a child, or moving to another city. A plan that is not designed to change will be challenged, ignored, and thrown out as unworkable within three months.

A financial plan will help you accomplish your goals. Whether those goals are balancing your budget, sending your children to college, or having secure finances in retirement, they will never be realized without a specific, intentional plan. A plan will help you allocate funds to meet those goals, while at the same time adding flexibility to individual and family expenses.

To be effective, a financial plan must have the support of all persons involved. If you are single, you have only yourself to contend with in your plan. If you get married and have children, your financial plan becomes more complex. Unless everyone, spouse and children alike, has some understanding of and acceptance of the financial plan, it will be a complete failure. A young child may not be able to understand all about financial planning, but you will be surprised how even young children can learn by, and understand, your financial situation. After all, what you teach them, directly and indirectly, as children will influence how they respond to money for the rest of their lives.

Best of all, a plan will allow you to meet financial emergencies and unexpected expenses without a nervous breakdown. Anyone who has stayed awake nights trying to figure how to send Jane to summer camp knows how a financial plan helps you sleep at night.

Why Financial Plans Fail

Without a plan, you are subject to the whims of each day, to your emotions, or to someone else's sales pitch rather than to faith, goals, and reason. Failure to plan may find you in bankruptcy court facing friends and the public with your failures. Without a plan, you will lack protection in the event of emergencies and catastrophes. (And they will happen, with or without a plan.) Without a plan, you may have to face your daughter on graduation eve and tell her that you cannot afford to send her to college. Without a plan, you may retire into a life of utter poverty.

37

If a financial plan is the cureall to financial disaster, why have so many failed at it? I have identified ten common causes for failure.

I'll do it tomorrow. Procrastination is the major culprit. It is the cause of most failures. "I know I must do it, but I have so many other things to do, and besides I'm tired. I'll do it tomorrow." Either tomorrow never comes, or when tomorrow does come you will find three other things to do first. As your financial plan takes shape, you will be amazed at how easy it is and how many other issues in your life will simply fall into place.

Fear of the future. "I don't know what tomorrow will bring. If I make a plan for the future, I just know I'm inviting something bad to happen." No one is certain about the future. I don't know what tomorrow will bring, but I know this: With a plan and with God, I can face anything tomorrow will bring. The Apostle Paul said something about that in Romans 8:31.

It is too complex. "I don't understand money. I never had a class on money, financial planning, or even budgeting." What we haven't tried is always complex and frightening. Follow the steps in this book, including answering the questions in each chapter, and you will find that financial planning is not a complex set of steps for someone with a master's degree in business administration but a simple plan to set you free.

I don't have much. The misunderstanding of financial planning is that only people with a lot of money need a financial plan. Another misconception is that if you don't have money to invest, you don't need a financial plan. No matter how much you have, if you have financial goals you want to accomplish, you cannot accomplish those goals without a plan.

Lack of vision. The failure to identify clear goals or a vision of what you want to accomplish will stall and eventually derail any financial plan. I have seen the simplest of plans die when someone involved in the plan asked, "Why are we doing this?"—and there was no real answer. Your vision of what you want to do will guide your plan and give reason to all you do.

Credit. Easy credit will be the downfall of any financial plan. Somehow we still think (whether as an individual or a nation) that if we charge it, we will not have to pay for it. Because of the importance of credit, and the debt that credit builds, I have devoted an entire chapter, "Dealing with Debt," to this problem.

Savings. This is both a goal and a problem. Without a systematic savings plan, even a simple $5.00 a week, your plan will begin to disintegrate the moment an emergency threatens your financial plan. The only way you will have any money in savings will be to start paying yourself out of *every* paycheck.

Records. Failure to keep careful records will undo your plan from the very start. Have you ever had a knit sweater with a loose thread? When you pull the thread, the sweater slowly unravels, until it is gone. So it is with records.

Even the simplest of recordkeeping, throwing bills in a shopping bag, is better than no records at all. Records will show where your money is going, will help reduce your tax burden, and will give you the necessary information to complete your financial plan.

Not seeking professional help. Most of us need a third party to help us accomplish our financial plan. The Nineties will be the decade of the financial planner. Whether that person is an insurance agent, a stockbroker, a CPA, a lawyer, or a certified financial planner, when you need the help of a professional, do not be afraid to seek that help. Most of these professionals cost less than you think, especially if they can help you accomplish your plan.

Leaving God out. Failure to include God in your plan will always spell disaster. Jesus calls to us in Luke 12 and reminds us that even as the lilies of the field and the birds of the air, so God will care for each of us. The early Hebrews discovered on their flight from bondage in Egypt to freedom in the Promised Land that God provided all they needed, each day. So it will be with us, as we include God in our daily plans.

Write down your reasons for not starting your plan today:

In prayer, give those excuses to God, and seek God's help in making this new plan work.

Most financial planning books begin with the process laid out in the remaining pages of this chapter. As Christians, we begin the financial planning process by recognizing and celebrating our relationship with God. We know that we cannot do anything without God. This is what sets this plan apart from most others. It is not just us trying to control our money, but a partnership with God in all we do. Through the Bible, God speaks to us

39

about money, teaching us values that should guide our financial plan. God's guidance includes:

Realize all your wealth comes from God.

1 Chronicles 29:11-16

Getting more is not the solution.

Ecclesiastes 5:10

Be content with what you have.

Philippians 4:11-12

Wealth is more than what you possess.

Luke 12:15

Be clear about your motives for spending.

1 John 2:15-16

Excessive debt is a call to slavery.

Proverbs 22:7

What other values does our Christian faith provide us for our financial plan?

Do I Need a Financial Plan?

Use the following checklist to test your need for a financial plan.

_____ I find it more and more difficult to pay the bills each month.

_____ In order to make ends meet, I need to work overtime or get a part-time job.

_____ When the bills come in, I can only pay the minimum due each month.

_____ I take cash advances on my credit card to pay bills.

_____ When taxes come due, I don't have enough money to pay my estimated tax. Or, before my tax refund check arrives, I have already spent it.

_____ I charge daily expenses now that I used to pay for with cash.

_____ I get past-due notices almost every month.

_____ I have children who want to go to college, but I haven't saved anything yet.

_____ I don't have any money in a savings or investment account.

_____ I don't have a will, or my will has not been revised in the last five years.

If you checked more than three boxes, you need a financial plan. Complete the rest of this financial planning process. If you checked more than six of these statements, you need the help of a financial planner or credit counseling center. If you checked fewer than three of these statements, congratulations—you are doing well. When you understand the principles in this book, you may want to help others.

Two Steps to Financial Freedom

The Christian financial planning process is an adventure in discovering and living out God's plan for your life. It is not God's plan for you to be a slave to your finances. Each step in the following process builds upon the previous step. Skip a step and you jeopardize your plan. Carefully study and implement each step and you will discover freedom and fun back in your life.

STEP ONE: IDENTIFY GOALS. Your financial plan is a road map in your journey through life. Sometimes while on a trip I am asked, "Where are we?" My flippant response is usually, "I don't know, but we're making good time." Is that the problem with your financial plan? You don't know where you are or where you are going, but you are moving along at a fast pace. A financial plan cannot get anywhere until you know for sure where you want to go. A financial plan is often discounted as a failure because without a destination in mind, such as a college education for Keri or a vacation next January in Florida, the work involved in the plan seems for nothing.

The first step in any trip is to decide where you want to go. That is called a goal. Let's see if we can discover your financial goals. Picture, if you will, a time in the future. It is your seventy-fifth birthday. Your family and friends are there celebrating with you a fulfilling and meaningful life. All you could ever hope for has happened. Describe what has happened in those years between now and your seventy-fifth birthday to make you feel successful with your financial plan:

NOTE: The financial planning process cannot be carried out in a vacuum. All persons in your immediate family who will be involved in your financial plan should be involved in each step of the process. To exclude anyone will put a kink in your plan that could derail all your hopes and dreams. Ask each person involved in your plan to write down her or his response to the previous situation. Compare your stories and combine them to describe an ideal future for you.

Now translate your vision of the ideal future into specific goals. This may not be all that easy at first. But it is essential in designing your plan. I find that most goals fall within these five major areas:

1. *Money management*—to be able to pay bills and live a comfortable life.
2. *College education*—to provide a college education for my children.
3. *Retirement*—to have adequate financial resources to live in retirement.
4. *Emergencies*—to provide for emergencies through contingency funds and insurance (health, disability, life).
5. *Tax*—to reduce tax obligations now and at death.

In addition, each plan has some goals that are specific to your plans. They might include:

1. To pay cash for our next car. Or, to pay at least 50 percent down and pay the balance in two years.
2. To go to Florida and spend a week in Orlando.
3. To buy a sailboat within two years.
4. To purchase a retirement home two years prior to retirement.

Goals are dreams with a plan. As you translate your vision into goals for your plan, be specific. The failure to accomplish your dreams may be tied to hazy goals. "I want a secure financial future" is a hazy goal. It may seem clear to you, but there is nothing specific on which to build your plan, to evaluate your plan, or to declare that you have accomplished this goal. Instead, your goal might state that by December 31 (year): we will have paid off all debt, except our home mortgage; we will be paying a minimum of a tithe; and we will be able to save 15 percent of my annual income each year. That is a big goal. But there are handles there on which to build your plan.

Your goals are changeable. Write down your goals as you see them today. Five years from now they may be different. They may be different because you have changed, because circumstances around you have changed, or because you have accomplished some of your goals. These goals will change and that is good. Your plan needs to be able to change with it.

Don't forget your faith goals as well as your personal goals. A faith goal may be to contribute a full tithe in eighteen months. Another faith goal may be to be part of a mission team for one week each year beginning no later than three years from now.

Write down as many specific goals as you can think of to accomplish your dream:

As you see your goals written down, maybe for the first time, how do you feel? It is exciting, isn't it, to be able to see the real possibility of accomplishing all that? Remember, all goals do not have to be accomplished in one year. There are short-range, medium-range, and long-range goals. In chapter seven you will put all your goals and dreams together into a life plan.

Next, look at your list of goals and prioritize them. Prioritization is nothing more than making a decision on *which goals* need to be accomplished in *what order*. Which should be first? The list does not necessarily mean a prioritization of importance. Of first importance to you may be sending your daughter to college in 2003. But you have $3,000 in credit card debt or your car has 112,000 miles on it. Doing something about these goals first makes the most sense. Which goals need to be accomplished, or at least begun, before other goals can be started? Write a number next to each goal corresponding to how you have prioritized them.

44

STEP TWO: IDENTIFY RESOURCES. Let's put aside your goals for a little while as you discover the resources available to accomplish these goals. You will come back to these goals in chapter seven on life planning. What resources do you have available that could be directed toward these goals?

Having the right tools available for your financial plan will make all the difference in the world. The first tool you need is a statement of net worth. It is a picture of your financial situation at a particular point in time. It is not a static picture. Each time you put together your statement it will be different. The picture drawn by this statement may surprise you. You will probably discover that you have more resources than you first thought. Focusing on what we owe, we often fail to take an inventory of what we have.

It will take some research to complete your first statement of net worth. It may take two or three hours the first time you do it. Each time thereafter it will be easier. The hardest part, the first time, is tracking down the information. Once you have the information, you can either update it the next time, or you will at least know where to find the information.

Don't take this task too lightly. Take all the time necessary to find the information. The information you uncover will help you in many ways:

1. It is a mirror image of your financial situation on any given day. Without this information, you will only guess at what you have. You will usually be wrong, and the wrong information could send your plan in the wrong direction.

2. It shows how well you are living your values. What you really believe will show up in your actions. Your statement of net worth, your checkbook, and your date book tell more about what is important to you than anything you may say.

3. Your statement of net worth will tell you which resources can be directed toward the accomplishment of your goals. Your home is not just a drain on your budget but may be a part of your overall retirement plan. The equity in your home may show possibilities for other goals on a short-term basis.

4. It is a barometer of how well you are accomplishing your plan. If one goal is to have $40,000 worth of assets available by the time your child starts college, you can see from your statement of net worth how well you are moving toward that goal at any specific time. Is your goal to increase the value of an investment? By comparing this year's statement to previous years you will be able to tell if your goal is being met.

5. It will show how well your assets are allocated. A person with average

45

income and few taxable assets may be foolish to invest in municipal bonds. One look at a couple's statement of net worth recently showed a high percentage of their assets in real estate. As they are approaching retirement, this distribution of their assets was inappropriate for their plan. Studying their statement of net worth, along with their goals, allowed us to realign their assets to meet those goals.

6. If you have ever completed a loan application for the purchase of a home, you know the anxiety produced through the simple act of gathering information. An updated statement of net worth will give you most of the information needed for a loan application. It will also impress the loan officer that you have such a statement. The remainder of the needed information is on the cash flow statement we will investigate next.

7. Finally, the statement of net worth is an invaluable tool in figuring your estate plan (chapter six). It will show, at a glance, what assets you have and how they should be allocated to avoid any unnecessary estate tax. In addition, it will help your surviving spouse, and/or administrator of your estate, to facilitate the accomplishment of your estate goals.

FORM 1
Our Net Worth
Joan & John B. Quick
December 31, 1990

Assets

Cash & Cash Equivalents

Checking	342
Savings	1,800
Money Market Funds	5,000
Total Cash & Cash Equivalents	$ 7,142

Invested Assets

Certificates of Deposit	10,000
Other Bank Accounts	–0–
Investment Accounts	7,500
Investment Property	–0–
Life Insurance (cash value)	3,400
Pension (amount vested)	19,342
Money Owed You	–0–
IRA Accounts	8,274
Miscellaneous Invested Assets	–0–
Total Invested Assets	$ 48,516

Use Assets

House	132,000
Second Home	–0–
Autos	18,000
Boat	2,400
Personal Property	
Household Furnishings	15,000
Personal Items	4,500
Miscellaneous Assets	–0–
Total Use Assets	$171,900

Total Assets

Cash & Cash Equivalents	7,142
Invested Assets	48,516
Use Assets	171,900
Total Assets	$227,558

Liabilities (what you owe)

Mortgage Balance	78,500
Auto Loan Balance	9,750
Credit Card Balance	349
Personal Loans	–0–
Bills Not Paid	871
Miscellaneous Debts	3,500
Total Liabilities	$ 92,970

Summary

Total Assets	227,558
Minus Total Liabilities	92,970
Total Net Worth	$134,588

Statement of Net Worth

Form 1 is a sample statement of net worth for Joan and John B. Quick. A statement of net worth is a listing of your assets (what you own) and your liabilities (what you owe). Subtract your liabilities from your assets and you have your net worth. Do not be alarmed if you do not include everything the first time. As soon as you complete your statement of net worth, you will discover something else you forgot. Don't be discouraged. See it as an adventure. Have fun!

Assets represent those items you own (even if you have a debt attached to them) which have the possibility of being sold or turned into cash. Just because something is valuable to you does not mean it has value for this statement. Aunt Betty's rocking chair may have great sentimental value to you, as it is filled with many fond memories. But if it were sold at auction, what would it bring?

All assets fall into three categories:

1. *Cash and cash equivalents*. These are cash balances in accounts you can get into immediately. They include checking accounts, savings accounts, money market accounts, even cash in a mattress or jar.

2. *Invested assets* are things you own for the purpose of investment growth. You can find the value of these assets in periodic statements you receive from real estate tax assessments, your CPA, brokerage statements, pension plan statements, or your life insurance agent. This will take some work, but it will give you a picture of yourself on any given day.

3. *Use assets* are all other assets you have which could be sold or otherwise turned into cash. This may be the most difficult of the three areas. Many items, such as your personal property, may be just a guess. Look at your insurance policy on your home. How much insurance do you carry on your personal property? If this is accurate, you can use this figure on your statement of net worth. The value of your cars, trucks, boats can be ascertained by using the annual NADA (National Automobile Dealers Association) listings at the library or a quick scan of the want ads to see what comparable vehicles are selling for.

Liabilities are all you owe. Your year-end statement from the mortgage company will show the balance you owe on your home. The bank, or lending agency, for your automobile can give you your current balance over the phone. Include all outstanding credit card balances and other debts you have as of the day of your report. Even include bills that are sitting with your

48

checkbook waiting to be paid. After all, we did include the checking account balance under assets.

Finally, subtract your liabilities (what you owe) from your assets (what you own), and you will have your net worth (what you are worth). If you haven't completed your statement of net worth, do it now!

How does this compare to the last time you did such a statement? Are you surprised at your net worth? What did you expect the figure to reveal?

What does this statement say about your values?

What part do your faith goals play in this statement?

What would you like to see different in your statement:

Six months from now?

One year from now?

Three years from now?

Five years from now?

Our Cash Flow
Joan & John B. Quick
December 31, 1990

Income

Income Joan*	$24,350	Social Security Income	–0–
Income John*	23,925	Partnership Income	–0–
Income Three	–0–	Business Income	–0–
Interest and Dividend	975	Gifts	–0–
Rental Income	–0–	Bonus	1,200
Pension Income	–0–	Other	500

Total Income $50,950

*After Tax Income

Fixed Expenses

Tithe	5,000	Installment Debt	
Savings	3,500	Auto 1	3,516
Mortgage/Rent	9,000	Auto 2	2,028
Insurance Life—1	921	Other	
Life—2	572	Allowance 1	1,100
Auto	1,200	2	1,100
Health	work	Children's Allowance 1	520
Disability	work	2	260
Home	mortgage		

Special Objectives Expenses

Reduction of Debt

Credit Cards	1,200
School Loan	708
Installment	–0–
Vacation Fund	2,000
Christmas Fund	750
Children's Education	1,500
Retirement	1,840

Variable Expenses

Food	4,975	Doctor	600
Clothing	1,500	Dentist	350
Utilities	2,040	Transportation	780
Electrical		Entertainment	820
Gas		Gifts	499
Water		Household Supplies	480
Telephone		Miscellaneous	1,691

Total Expenses $50,950

Cash Flow Statement

You will need your checkbook from last year for this next step in your plan. Form 2 is a cash flow statement for Joan and John B. Quick. This is a record of their income and expenses for the past year. The cash flow statement is an annual report of income and expenditures. It will give you an overall picture of where your money goes. From this picture of yourself you will be able to decide where you can make changes in your spending habits in order to accomplish your goals. The first time you work on your cash flow statement, you may have to estimate many of these figures. The information gathered in this form will not only give you a picture of last year's expenses, but will be the foundation upon which your spending plan will be built for next year.

Begin by listing all sources of income. If you get a pay stub, use it to figure your after-tax income. As a last resort, you can always rely on last year's W-2, 1099, and 1040 tax forms for this information. Include all sources of income. Don't forget about the fifty dollars Aunt Sue sends each year for your birthday. That is income. It may not be taxable income, but it is income nonetheless. Joan receives a bonus each year, so she included that on her statement. John does odd jobs in the neighborhood once in a while, so he included the $500 he estimates he made last year.

All of your expenses will fall into three categories.

1. *Fixed Expenses*—Those expenditures which are predictable in time and amount.
2. *Special Objectives Expense*—This category shows that Joan and John had chosen special objectives last year. They can compare these results with their goals. This category may well change each year.
3. *Variable Expenses*—This is where all other expenses will fit. Spending in this category varies in time and amount. The first year you do this may be difficult. It will get easier. Make the line items in this category fit your needs and spending habits. Do not try to force all of your expenses into the same categories as John and Joan. This is their statement and is used only as an example.

52

As you review your Cash Flow Statement, what does it tell you?

Do your expenditures reflect what you believe to be important and of value to your life?

What line items are higher than you would have thought? What line items are lower than you expected? Describe why these items are out of line with your expectations.

How do your expenditures for last year reflect your Christian faith?

Before you go further in the financial planning process, free yourself from overwhelming debt. The single most damaging enemy of your financial plan will be debt. Some debt is good. Overwhelming debt, debt that derails your financial plan, debt that makes you uncomfortable, will undoubtedly challenge all your plans for life. Before any other goals can be met in your financial plan, overwhelming debt must be controlled.

If overwhelming debt is a problem, do not use credit cards for any purchase until your debt is under control. I know there is always an excuse to charge something. Your best strategy is to lock your credit cards away somewhere and not use them.

Because of the importance of this area to your overall financial plan, I have chosen to make it a separate chapter. If debt is your major worry today, place a marker in this page, read the chapter on debt (chapter five) and then return to this page.

~ ~
~ ~
~ ~
~ ~
~ ~

CHAPTER FOUR
DESIGN A PLAN FOR SPENDING

Of this gospel I have become a servant according to the gift of God's grace that was given me by the working of his power. Although I am the very least of all the saints, this grace was given me to bring to the Gentiles the news of boundless riches of Christ, and to make everyone see what is the plan of the mystery hidden for ages in God who created all things (Ephesians 3:7-9).

By the twenty-second day of the month do you wonder where the money has gone? The checkbook has no balance, the wallet is just as empty as the refrigerator, and there are still eight days to go before payday. Are you surprised on April 15, when you are finishing your taxes, to discover that you earned so much this past year? Where has it gone? Why don't we have something to show for it? We need help!

Sharon was my first wife. That is, she and I were "married" (actually assigned to each other) during an economics class in our senior year in high school. As a family (husband and wife), we were to design our budget and financial plans. At the beginning of the class project we were given an envelope. Within the envelope was a description of our lives: educational background, age, how long we had been married, income, and other information about our economic situation. With this information we were to design our money plan.

Periodically we were given extra envelopes with conditions that changed our economic situation (birth of the first child, serious illness, substantial raise, loss of employment, etc.). Once each week we were to report in class how our budget would respond to each of these changes. As I approached adult responsibilities with money, this was the only formal training I ever had in money management. Many of us did not even have that much.

I don't like budgets! They never seem to work. Like a diet, a budget seems to constantly remind me that I have already failed. No matter how well I use those budget books I get down at the bookstore, money seems to have a mind of its own. Besides, a budget keeps reminding me of what I cannot do.

Budget is a dirty word in some households. It is considered a four-letter word. Mention it and you will get your mouth washed out with soap. How do

55

you respond to the word *budget?* Describe your experiences with using a budget.

Instead of a budget, which describes what I cannot do, I prefer a SPENDING PLAN. A spending plan describes what I can do! It describes what I am already doing. I am spending! It gives me some control, allows me to make some decisions, and gives me some hope that my spending will help accomplish some of my vision for the future. I find that budgets don't work but spending plans do!

A spending plan is a journey toward financial freedom. It is a road map designed to lead you toward your goals. It shows you have a vision of certain desired results. It is a pattern for your behavior on that journey. It will free you from past habits you want to change. It will free you from controls imposed by the limits of more month left at the end of your money. It will help you set the parameters by which decisions are made. It is a sign pointing to what can be. It is a sign declaring how you will respond to God's call in your life.

Give yourself three months using what is described in this chapter, and your money plan will show results. Give the plan a year, and you will see some of your goals actually showing signs of being accomplished. Make this your life plan, as explained in chapter seven, and you will discover new freedom and excitement in seeing your, and God's, plan for your life coming true.

56

God and you are partners in financial planning, from the very beginning. Like the rich farmer in Luke 12:16-21, if you rely only on yourself, no matter what you do, you will eventually fail.

What are five things you will do to make this plan a partnership between God and you?

1.

2.

3.

4.

5.

From the very beginning, all persons involved in this plan must be part of the decision-making process. I remember an early attempt to design our spending plan. My wife and I had figured what our spending plan would be. Then the boys would want some expensive tennis shoes or hightops of some kind. Then they wanted new jeans. Then something else. There is no way you can plan for all contingencies, but you can come close.

My wife, our two boys, and I sat down and figured how much each spent on clothes during a year. We agreed on an amount (an allowance) each could spend on clothes in a year. Then we divided that amount by twelve months. Each month we would contribute an amount to a fund for clothes. Each person had a sheet in our record book upon which deposits and expenditures were recorded for clothing. (No one could spend their clothing allowance higher than their balance.) So, if the boys wanted a $75 pair of shoes, because everyone else had those shoes, they checked their balances. If it was low, they waited until their balance allowed them to purchase whatever they needed. The extra wait to purchase the item often gave them the needed time to rethink their purchase. They changed their minds more than I imagined they would. But not always. They made the decisions. As parents, we were out of the controlling role. Instead of a budget, we had a plan for spending. Before asking, they checked the spending plan.

Take time with your spending plan. It will not take more than an hour or so a week at first. As you progress further and feel more comfortable with your plan, it will take less time. But don't give up. What is being developed is a lifelong process. Your plan is unique to you. You bring to your plan years of conditioning. It will take time to build a plan that will work for you.

Be careful not to make your plan rigid. Be flexible! If you make your spending plan so tight that there is no room for change, at the first emergency, you will give up. You will abandon your plan as another failure. Be ready to make changes when changes are needed.

Take Charge

Next, after you and God have entered into this partnership, it is important to take charge of your spending plan. Determine that you will make this plan work. Decide that you will give it at least three months. And that you *will* work at it during those three months. Be clear and realistic about what you want to see accomplished with your spending plan. "In six months, I want to get a handle on my spending. I want to know where my money goes." "Within three months I want to be able to get my debt repayment on a regular schedule. I want to see my debt paid off in two years, so I can get on with my life."

What three specific goals do you want to accomplish with your spending plan in the next year?

1.

2.

3.

Someone needs to be the financial manager. If you are single and you need help, select a close friend to work with you on your spending plan. If you are married, one of you needs to be the manager of the financial plan. That person is not a guard or a police officer enforcing the plan. If you still need help, do not be afraid to seek help from a certified financial planner.

In deciding which person should be manager, consider which of you has the most knowledge, time, or ability around managing the plan. If you decide to do it together, without anyone in charge, after a while your plan will be abandoned. Someone needs to be in charge of your plan. Decide now, together, who will be the manager of this spending plan. Remember, the plan belongs to both of you (and the children, too). Make this a three-month decision. At the end of three months, evaluate the role of manager and renegotiate the responsibility for another three months.

Take charge of your spending. The problem for many of us is that we do not know where our money goes. It just disappears. Record every cent that is spent for the next three months. Each person will record daily how much he/she spends and for what. Weekly (not weakly) the manager will gather this information into categories (food, gas, utilities, eating out, etc.) and record the total amount spent. One family I worked with kept track of their spending. They were surprised at what they discovered. They never seemed to have money to accomplish their goals. When they kept track of their spending, they discovered they spent $400 a month on what they called "unnecessary expenses."

Janie and Luis discovered that they were spending $210 a month at quick stop markets. In their rush to leave home each morning, they never stopped to make lunch. So they stopped at the deli counter at the market for a cup of coffee to go and a sandwich for lunch.

When Sue tried keeping an account of where her money went, she discovered she was spending $50 a month on soda and snacks at work. Since savings was one of her goals, she cut her snacks back to $25 a month and saved the rest. She now has $500 in a savings account that she never had before.

Take charge of your spending. By keeping a careful account, you will increase your awareness of where your money is being spent. Pinpoint areas where you can change your spending habits. Decide what you will do with the money you save. If you could save $25 a month, what would you do with your savings?

Develop Your Spending Plan

See the whole picture. Each month's spending is not just one-twelfth of the yearly plan. Each month is different. Using your cash flow statement (page 116) and your record of spending for a three-month period, design your spending plan. Create your spending plan in the same way Joan and John B. Quick have done in the following example. (A blank form is provided in the appendix for your use. You are given permission to copy this form, for your personal use only.) Study the Quicks' spending plan on the next several pages. Then read on to discover how you can develop your own plan.

Our Spending Plan
Joan & John B. Quick
Jan.-June 1991

Income	Annual Budget	January Budget	January Spent	February Budget	February Spent	March Budget	March Spent	April Budget	April Spent	May Budget	May Spent	June Budget	June Spent
Income One JOAN	25812	2151		2151		2151		2151		2151		2151	
Income Two JOHN	24900	2075		2075		2075		2075		2075		2075	
Income Three													
Interest and Dividend	990									425			
Rental Income													
Pension Income													
Social Security Income													
Partnership Income													
Business Income													
Gifts													
Bonus	1200												
Other	500											125	
Total Income	53402	4226		4226		4226		4226		4651		4351	

Our Spending Plan
July-Dec. 1991

Income	July Budget	July Spent	August Budget	August Spent	September Budget	September Spent	October Budget	October Spent	November Budget	November Spent	December Budget	December Spent	Annual Budget	Annual Spent
Income One	2151		2151		2151		2151		2151		2151		25812	
Income Two	2075		2075		2075		2075		2075		2075		24900	
Income Three														
Interest and Dividend									565				990	
Rental Income														
Pension Income														
Social Security Income														
Partnership Income														
Business Income														
Gifts														
Bonus							1200						1200	
Other	185		190										500	
Total Income	4411		4416		4226		5426		4791		4226		53402	

Our Spending Plan
Jan.-June 1991

Fixed Expenses	Annual Budget	January Budget	January Spent	February Budget	February Spent	March Budget	March Spent	April Budget	April Spent	May Budget	May Spent	June Budget	June Spent
Tithe	5500	425		425		425		425		475		435	
Savings	4200	350		350		350		350		350		350	
Mortgage/Rent	9000	750		750		750		750		750		750	
Insurance Life—1	921					460							
Life—2	572							286					
Auto	1310							655					
Health	—												
Disability	—												
Home	—												
Installment Debt													
Auto 1	3516	293		293		293		293		293		293	
Auto 2	2028	169		169		169		169		169		169	
School													
Other													
Allowance 1	900	75		75		75		75		75		75	
2	900	75		75		75		75		75		75	
Children's Allowance	780	65		65		65		65		65		65	
2	390	32.50		32.50		32.50		32.50		32.50		32.50	
Total Fixed Expenses	30017	2294.50		2234.50		2694.50		3175.50		2284.50		2294.50	

Our Spending Plan
July-Dec. 1991

Fixed Expenses	July Budget	July Spent	August Budget	August Spent	September Budget	September Spent	October Budget	October Spent	November Budget	November Spent	December Budget	December Spent	Annual Budget	Annual Spent
Tithe	450		450		425		665		475		425		5500	
Savings	350		350		350		350		350		350		4200	
Mortgage/Rent	750		750		750		750		750		750		9000	
Insurance Life—1					461								921	
Life—2							286						572	
Auto							655						1310	
Health														
Disability														
Home														
Installment Debt														
Auto 1	293		293		293		293		293		293		3516	
Auto 2	169		169		169		169		169		169		2028	
School														
Other														
Allowance 1	75		75		75		75		75		75		900	
2	75		75		75		75		75		75		900	
Children's Allowance	65		65		65		65		65		65		780	
2	32.50		32.50		32.50		32.50		32.50		32.50		390	
Total Fixed Expenses	2259.50		2259.50		2695.50		3415.50		2284.50		2234.50		30017	

Our Spending Plan
Jan.-June 1991

This Year's Special Objectives	Annual Budget	January Budget	January Spent	February Budget	February Spent	March Budget	March Spent	April Budget	April Spent	May Budget	May Spent	June Budget	June Spent
Reduction of Debt													
Credit Cards	900	75		75		75		75		75		75	
School Loan	708	59		59		59		59		59		59	
Installment	600	50		50		50		50		50		50	
Vacation Fund	2400												
Christmas Fund	900	475											
Children's Education	1800	150		150		150		150		150		150	
Retirement	1860	155		155		155		155		155		155	
Total Special Objectives	9168	964		489		489		489		489		489	

Our Spending Plan
July-Dec. 1991

This Year's Special Objectives	July		August		September		October		November		December		Annual	
	Budget	Spent	Budget	Spent	Budget	Spent	Budget	Spent	Budget	Spent	Budget	Spent	Budget	Spent
Reduction of Debt														
Credit Cards	75		75		75		75		75		75		900	
School Loan	59		59		59		59		59		59		708	
Installment	50		50		50		50		50		50		600	
Vacation Fund	1500		900										2400	
Christmas Fund											425		900	
Children's Education	150		150		150		150		150		150		1800	
Retirement	155		155		155		155		155		155		1860	
Total Special Objectives	1989		1389		489		489		489		914		9168	

Our Spending Plan
Jan.-June 1991

Variable Expenses	Annual Budget	January Budget	January Spent	February Budget	February Spent	March Budget	March Spent	April Budget	April Spent	May Budget	May Spent	June Budget	June Spent
Food	5040	390		390		390		390		390		390	
Clothing	1800	150		25								300	
Utilities	2200												
Electrical		55		60		50		50		45		70	
Gas		85		90		70		43		15		13	
Water		15		15		18		25		18		45	
Telephone		45		45		45		45		45		45	
Doctor	600	200		100		100							
Dentist	350	125						50		50		50	
Transportation	1020	85		85		85		85		85		85	
Entertainment	900	75		75		75		75		75		75	
Gifts	350							15		100			
Household supplies	580	50		50		50		50		50		45	
Taxes—Local & State													
Federal													
Social Security													
Emergencies	600	50		50		50		50		50		50	
Miscellaneous	777	65		65		65		65		65		65	
Total Variable Expenses	14217	1390		1050		998		1003		988		1233	

Our Spending Plan
July-Dec. 1991

Variable Expenses	July Budget	July Spent	August Budget	August Spent	September Budget	September Spent	October Budget	October Spent	November Budget	November Spent	December Budget	December Spent	Annual Budget	Annual Spent
Food	300		390		420		390		600		600		5040	
Clothing					500						400		1800	
Utilities													2200	
Electrical	90		90		70		55		70		75			
Gas	13		21		27		35		38		70			
Water	60		60		45		18		23		18			
Telephone	45		45		45		45		45		45			
Doctor							50				50		600	
Dentist	125								50				350	
Transportation	85		85		85		85		85		85		1020	
Entertainment	75		75		75		75		75		75		900	
Gifts					100				75				350	
Household supplies	35		50		50		50		50		50		580	
Taxes — Local & State														
Federal														
Social Security														
Emergencies	50		50		50		50		50		50		600	
Miscellaneous	65		63		65		65		65		65		777	
Total Variable Expenses	943		929		1532		918		1226		1583		14217	

Our Spending Plan
Jan.-June 1991

Summary	Annual Budget	January	February	March	April	May	June
Total Income	53402	4226	4226	4226	4226	4651	4351
Expenses							
Fixed Expenses	30017	2234.50	2234.50	2694.50	3175.50	2284.50	2244.50
Special Objectives	9168	964	489	489	489	489	489
Variable Expenses	14217	1390	1050	998	1003	988	1233
Total Expenses	53402	4388.50	3773.50	4181.50	4667.50	3761.50	3966.50
Difference	-0-	-162.50	+452.50	+44.50	-441.50	+889.50	+384.50

Our Spending Plan
July-Dec. 1991

Summary	July	August	September	October	November	December	Annual Totals
Total Income	4411	4416	4226	5426	4791	4226	53 402
Expenses							
Fixed Expenses	2259.50	2259.50	2695.50	3415.50	2284.50	2234.50	30,017
Special Objectives	1989	1389	489	489	489	914	9168
Variable Expenses	943	929	1532	918	1226	1583	14217
Total Expenses	5190.50	4577.50	4716.50	4822.50	3999.50	4731.50	53402
Difference	-779.50	-161.50	-490.50	+603.50	+791.50	-505.50	—0—

Now it is time for you to work on your own plan. You will need the blank forms in the appendix (pp. 118-127). Make several photocopies of each form in case you need to start over or adjust your information.

STEP ONE: Record your income from all sources. Some amounts may have to be estimated. Joan and John's income is fixed each month. They know they can count on one-twelfth of their salary (after taxes) each month. If your income is irregular, because of a seasonal job or because of commissions, use your income from last year to estimate your monthly income. Income from interest and dividends comes at different times of the year. All sources of income should be included in your plan. John does odd jobs each summer and earns $500. Joan gets a bonus. What income do you receive beyond your salary? Record that income in the month you expect it. If you get a tax refund check each year in May, record that estimated amount as part of your income plan. When you total each month, you will notice that your income is not the same each month.

STEP TWO: Record your expected spending for the next year, as did Joan and John. You can find this information from your cash flow statement from last year, your checkbook record, and your three-month spending record. Each year is different. What new expenses do you expect this year? Will your vacation plans be different from last year? As I worked on my plan this year, I knew I would have extra expenses for my son's class ring and my nephew's wedding. If I just adopted last year's plan, I would not be ready for these new demands on my spending. It is easier on your emotional and financial well-being to think through these situations before they challenge your plan. Think about your new year. What different things will impinge on your spending plan? Record your planned expenditures in three categories: fixed expenses, special objectives, and variable expenses.

Fixed expenses are those items that are predictable both in amount and time. Most of these items will be the same each month. Rent or mortgage payments, auto loan payments, and other installment debts are repaid on a regular basis. Insurance payments are also predictable in amount and time but are not usually a monthly expense. Without a spending plan, you will be surprised, as I was one year, when the life insurance payment was due in November and I didn't have the money. Notice that your tithe and savings are in the category of fixed expenses. A Christian's goal is to tithe, or to contribute a proportionate share of what is earned. After your tithe, pay yourself! Select an amount and put it in your savings each pay period.

Special objectives are those expenditures, even if they are to a savings account, that coincide with special plans you have for this year. The Quicks' special objectives are to pay off debt and save for a vacation, Christmas gifts, the children's education, and retirement. This is where they recorded their plans. Be realistic and flexible with these special objectives. Some months you

71

may be able to do more than other months. Joan and John are planning to spend (or save) the same amount each month toward their goals, except for the Christmas and vacation fund. You may want to set aside different amounts in different months according to your total plan.

Variable expenses are those expenses that may change in amount each month. In this category you will record all expenses not found in any other category. *Variable* means that the amount of expenditure may change month by month. It may also mean that some of these categories are subject to more control on your part. You cannot do much to change your rent or mortgage, except by moving. You may be able to do something to reduce your utilities, your spending for food, yes, even your taxes. We will look at some ways to improve your spending in chapter five which discusses debt. This may be the hardest category to figure. Remember, this is a spending plan. As you work with it, you are allowed to make changes. You can even reconstruct your plan any time you wish. The longer your work with this plan, the easier it will be.

STEP THREE: Using the summary sheets, summarize your income and expenses for each month. The first thing you will notice is that every month is different. In the example of Joan and John B. Quick, not one month's income balance is the same. Some months you will spend more than you earn. On the other hand, there will be months that you will earn more than you spend. Do not worry about balancing income and expenditures each month.

Look through your plan. In those months that expenditures are higher than income, can you rearrange any of your spending to other months? Can you shift any expenses, in whole or in part, to months where income is higher? When you have made changes and your spending plan does not balance, don't give up hope. You have just discovered the secret of the overall picture. In the past, if there was any money left after all your bills were paid, what did you do? Did you leave it in the checkbook? If you did, you spent it, right? A balance in the checkbook is an invitation to spend. In reality, the balance is not extra money. The overall picture shows that a balance this month is needed to cover the shortfall next month or two months from now. It is not extra money. In those months that you have a balance, put the extra money in a savings account for those out-of-balance months.

Don't be surprised if your first attempt at a spending plan shows you spending more than you earn. You have discovered the second secret of the spending plan. Without a spending plan, you go on spending. Without a spending plan, you have no awareness of how much you have coming in or where it goes. Without the awareness a spending plan offers, you will keep spending and sink deeper in debt.

If your spending plan shows you spending more than you earn, you will have to make some changes. You have three choices: You can go on spending

72

until you are hopelessly in debt, you can go out and get a job that pays more or a second job to increase your income, or you can change your spending habits. The place to start is to review your spending plan. Don't go wild and begin chopping away at your plan. If you do, you will give up in total defeat.

Gather all persons involved in your plan. Explain the situation. It is not a problem. Calling it a problem puts everyone on the defensive. It is an *opportunity* to be in control of your spending before a potential disaster spoils all your plans. Where can you change your spending plan? Are some of your expenditures estimated higher than you may actually spend? Are some of your spending plans unrealistic? Creative solutions and sincere ownership of the plan will evolve from these discussions.

How does your spending plan compare with other spending plans? I am always hesitant to answer that question. Every person's or family's plan is different. But there are similarities. The following tables are for comparison only. The figures represent percentages of annual income. These represent before-tax situations and are expressed as a percentage of annual income.

ANNUAL SPENDING PLAN GUIDELINES

Family Size Age Annual Income	Single No Kids 25 $25,000	Married No Kids 30 $35,000	Married 2 Kids 40 $45,000	Married No Kids 55 $55,000	Married No Kids 65 $35,000	Single No Kids 65 + $30,000
Housing	27%	26%	23%	23%	23%	22%
Food	12%	13%	11%	11%	13%	12%
Clothing	3%	4%	5%	5%	4%	3%
Transportation	10%	10%	9%	9%	10%	10%
Medical	3%	4%	3%	3%	5%	5%
Insurance	2%	3%	3%	3%	4%	3%
Recreation	5%	6%	5%	5%	6%	5%
Gifts	2%	2%	2%	2%	2%	2%
Debt	4%	4%	4%	4%	4%	4%
Other	4%	5%	8%	8%	5%	5%
Federal, State, Local Taxes	28%	23%	27%	28%	24%	28%

*These figures adapted from *Personal Financial Planning*, Practitioners Publishing Co.; Fort Worth, TX, 1989. Reprinted with permission.

Joan and John B. Quick found the spending plan to be a perfect way to see an annual picture of their spending plan. But they still needed some tool to help them with their everyday spending. They tried a monthly budget and found it hard. They didn't get paid by the month but twice a month. They took their spending plan and made a *paycheck spending plan.*

I have found it helpful in my own spending plan to create a paycheck spending plan for each pay period, whether monthly, weekly, or whenever I get paid. Assign specific expenditures to each pay period. That way you will know how each paycheck is to be spent. In essence, you will have a separate spending plan for each pay period.

STEP FOUR: Constantly review your spending plan. The longer you let your plan go without review, the greater the potential for problems. For the first two years, review your plan at least quarterly. After the first two years, the plan will come naturally to you and will not need to be reviewed quite as often. Evaluate your plan at least once each year. A good time to do this is between Christmas and New Year's. Use this time to evaluate the plan for the past year and design your plan for the coming year.

Changes to your plan are inevitable. With your plan, you will be prepared to deal with the unexpected. Secret three of your spending plan is that changes are permitted. When an unexpected expense occurs, and it will, act on it. Plan for an emergency or unexpected expense each month. If that budget item is not needed, put it in a savings account for future emergencies. Build up your emergency fund to one month's income as a start. Most financial planners suggest having three to six months' income in an emergency fund. That's great! But if you are just beginning your plan, go for one month's income.

If an expenditure is necessary, look at your overall spending plan to see where you can reduce your spending for this month to cover the unexpected expense. It may take several months to pay for those new tires on the car that you had hoped would last another six months. Reducing expenditures or postponing a purchase will help put your spending plan under your control.

As you work with your spending plan, let me make a few more suggestions:

Make room in your plan to enjoy yourself. If you enjoy going out to dinner some place besides a fast food restaurant or to the theater for the newest movie, plan on it. If your spending plan is so tight that you and your spouse, or a friend, cannot enjoy yourselves, the plan will become a burden and you will soon abandon it. Don't go overboard; be realistic, but reward yourself once in a while.

JOAN & JOHN B. QUICK
PAYCHECK SPENDING PLAN
FEBRUARY

February 1

	Budget	Actual
Income	$2113.00	
Expenditures		
Tithe	200.00	
Savings	175.00	
Mortgage	750.00	
Auto Loan	169.00	
Allowance	123.75	
Education Fund	150.00	
Food	195.00	
Utility: Water	15.00	
Transportation	40.00	
Entertainment	25.00	
Supplies	15.00	
Emergencies and Misc.	50.00	
Future Bills (to Savings)	205.25	

February 15

	Budget	Actual
Income	$2113.00	
Expenditures		
Tithe	225.00	
Savings	175.00	
Auto Loan	293.00	
Allowance	123.75	
Credit Cards	75.00	
School Loan	59.00	
Installment	50.00	
Retirement	155.00	
Food	195.00	
Clothing	25.00	
Electric	60.00	
Gas	90.00	
Phone	45.00	
Doctor	100.00	
Transportation	45.00	
Entertainment	50.00	
Supplies	35.00	
Emergencies and Misc.	65.00	
Future Bills (to Savings)	247.25	

Make savings a priority. After paying your tithe, pay yourself. Money in a savings account is a goal for everyone with whom I have worked. Another secret of the spending plan is that we spend to our limit. If you earn $2,000 a month, you will spend $2,000. But, if you take $100 out of that and put it in a savings account, you will not miss the $100. After a year, you will have $1,200, plus approximately $45 in interest. If you can put $5 away each pay period, and you get paid twice a month, you will have $120 plus interest at the end of a year.

If savings is one of your goals, the answer comes in systematic payments to yourself. Don't spend a raise, a tax refund, or a gift of cash. Put it in your savings and enjoy the excitement of seeing one of your goals being accomplished.

Pay everyone an allowance. An allowance is an amount given to each person. The amount for each may be different, according to each person's circumstances. An allowance is money for which the individual does not have to be accountable. They can save or spend it in any way they wish.

I don't like diets, but once in a while I need to be on one. I have tried all kinds of diets. Sometimes they work, and sometimes they do not. If a diet is going to work, there are certain things I must do. Like a diet, if your spending plan is going to work for you, there are certain things required of you.

Commitment—For your plan to succeed, you, and everyone involved in the plan, must be totally committed to it.

Plan—You must have a written plan. This is important both to you and to others. You must know what you are going to do. Just hoping you will spend less, save more, or have more is not enough. You must know where you are going and how you will get there. A written plan will allow you to evaluate your progress.

Time—It has taken you a long time to get where you are in your finances. It will take time to get spending under control.

Change lifestyle—Part of your current financial situation is the result of the way you live. You may have to evaluate your lifestyle for changes beneficial to your financial plan.

Exercise—This is the hardest part of a plan. Work at your plan and your plan will pay you rich dividends.

Enjoy the results—Getting in control of your finances is exciting and fun. Seeing your goals beginning to materialize is worth all the changes, cutbacks, and work your plan requires.

CHAPTER FIVE
DEALING WITH DEBT

A man is rich in proportion to the number of
things which he can afford to leave alone.
                              Henry David Thoreau

[Jesus said,] "Take care! Be on your guard
against all kinds of greed; for one's life does not
consist in the abundance of possessions."
                              Luke 12:15

Bob pulled me aside following a meeting. In a dark corner of the room, he whispered so no one else could hear, "I'm in trouble. I have $8,000 in credit card bills, and I don't know what to do!" He proceeded to tell me his story. He had always had an ongoing balance on his credit cards. It was never a large balance. He accepted credit card debt as part of life. There was this cruise his wife, Darlene, wanted to go on with friends from the Sunday school. Several couples were going, and it seemed like it would be fun. Not having the money, they charged it on their credit card. It was even more fun than they imagined. It was also very relaxing. It was just what Bob needed!

The plan was to pay off the cruise over the next six months. Then Bob's mother got sick, and he felt he needed to fly up to be with her. He charged the airfare and car rental to one of his cards. When he came back two weeks later the credit card statement was waiting for him. There was a $3,500 balance. The minimum due was only $125. Paying the minimum was easy. Over the next three months he paid twice the minimum and was feeling good about getting the balance paid. Then his daughter, Sue, came over one night and announced she and Bill were going to get married. Sue was their only daughter, and Bill was going to be a great son-in-law.

Everyone congratulated them on how beautiful Sue's dress looked at the wedding and how wonderful the reception was. What they didn't know was how much of the wedding went on a charge card.

Just as Bob reached the limit on his credit card, the limit would be raised. Since he had charged so much, other credit card companies sent him applications for their card. "It got to the point," he shared, "that I could only pay the minimum due on the cards. Then I was so depressed that I would go out and charge more than I paid on the credit card balance. Do

77

you know that the interest alone is $153 a month? Between those credit cards, the auto loans, the mortgage, and other bills, there is no money left to buy food." Bob wiped away a tear as he continued, "Darlene doesn't know anything about our situation. What should I do?"

Bob's situation is becoming more and more common. Individuals, corporations, and even governments have learned how to overuse credit. The number one enemy of any financial plan is the abuse of credit.

Over the past twenty years, the use of credit has become "standard operating procedure." At times of high inflation and rapid increases in the cost of living, we were taught to buy now and pay later. We were shown how it would take fewer working hours tomorrow to pay today's debt. And we would be making more money tomorrow. (I question that philosophy.) If it did make sense in the Seventies and Eighties, it does not make sense in the Nineties. With inflation "under control," or at least less than it was in the Seventies, prices will not escalate as fast. The cost-of-living, and corresponding increases to our earnings, will not see the rapid increases of the past twenty years. All these factors encourage a save-now-buy-later philosophy. Yet, we are still caught up with the desire to "charge it."

Credit is not the problem! There are situations where the use of credit and the accompanying debt is appropriate. The purchase of a home, some transportation purchases, and credit card charges which can be paid in full when they come due, are some examples of acceptable uses of credit. The purchase of something whose value increases or whose balance due is never more than its value may also be appropriate uses of credit. Credit cards are often needed to cash checks and for identification. It is also easier to rent a car and register in a hotel if you have a credit card. There is also security in having credit in times of emergency. Credit has its appropriate uses, if the accompanying debt is paid in a planned and timely manner.

There are times when the use of credit actually makes sense. Some credit is actually a savings plan. If you buy something on credit and pay for it in two to three years, and there is value left when the item is paid off, you may actually be ahead of the game. Antwan and LaNita could not save. No matter how hard they tried, they had no savings. A bank friend of theirs convinced them to take out a loan for $1,000 for a year. When they got the $1,000 they placed it in a one-year certificate of deposit. Each month they repaid the bank for the loan. At the end of the year, the loan was paid and they had $1,075 in a savings account. Their spending plan never missed the $95 monthly payments. Now they are paying themselves $100 each month.

I would not go as far as the Apostle Paul when he wrote to the Roman church, "Owe no one anything" (Rom. 13:8). Paul is speaking specifically about taxes. He says that we should pay them as part of our citizenship. But beyond that, Paul is making a good point. "Owe no one anything." Let no one put you in financial bondage. Let no one have a claim on your life,

78

except Christ. In the wisdom literature of Proverbs (22:7) we see a picture painted of a borrower as a "slave of the lender."

As Christians we hear Jesus' warning about greed (Luke 12:15). Greed is the insatiable desire to acquire more. For some people this desire runs out of control and leads to overwhelming debt. The vicious circle is even more out of control in our day because of easy credit. Overextended debt obligates you to someone other than God. If you have to work overtime, perhaps thirty hours a week, or even work two jobs, in order to extend your credit and acquire extras, you have obligated yourself to someone, or something—your debt. Your life is no longer yours. You suffer, your family suffers, and your relationship to God suffers. Remember what Jesus said about not serving both God and mammon?

Everyone has certain months or a period of time when spending will be greater than income. Credit allows us to live through those periods of time. If handled well, the use of credit may be an integral part of a financial plan. When debt makes us a slave to those we owe, then we have abused credit. How can I know if I am a slave to debt?

Am I a Slave to Debt?

How many of the following statements are true about your financial plan?

A. Your monthly expenditures are higher than your income.

B. You are surprised when the credit card statement is received. You did not know that you had charged that much.

C. You cannot pay the entire balance due on your credit card for three consecutive months.

D. You can pay only the minimum balance due on your credit cards.

E. Because you cannot pay the minimum, you do not even attempt to pay any part of the credit card balance. (You think, maybe if you put it in a drawer a little gnome will pay it.)

F. When you add up all your debt (excluding the mortgage payment), you owe 15 percent or more of your after-tax income for debt repayment.

G. In order to have money until the next pay period, you get a cash advance from your credit card.

H. You get past-due notices on bills.

I. You have a negative net worth (your liabilities are higher than your assets).

J. You take out new loans to repay existing loans.

K. Your savings account balance is less than $500.

L. You use credit for items you used to buy with cash.

M. You are anxious about the amount of debt you owe.

N. The only way to stay solvent is to work overtime or get a second job (for you and/or your spouse).

If you answered true to four of more of these statements, then you are a slave to debt. The reduction of your debt load should be your first financial goal.

Factors Leading to Debt Overload

"If I only had $150 more a month," Bob declared, "I could solve all my problems." I have heard similar statements from people in all walks of life. No matter if you make $175 a week or $100,000 a year, "a little bit more" will not solve your financial problems. Before we look at some steps to take to relieve "debt-stress," it is important to know how we got ourselves into this situation. Besides not having enough money, why do you think you are experiencing debt overload?

Knowing why you are in the present situation is a good step forward in climbing out of the debt-overload pit. If you can figure out what you did to get to this point and then change your financial habits, you will find yourself on the road to recovery in no time at all. The following are the most common reasons people get over-their-heads in debt.

Failure to set goals. The failure to set financial goals is the problem in most financial planning failures. Without specific and attainable goals, there is no guidance to the financial plan. Without goals there is no direction to guide your spending or your savings.

Lack of information. The more monetary our culture becomes, the more information is needed to manage even the simplest financial plan. When money was scarce for everyone, when wants were minimal, financial information was not needed. As our economic life as a society increases and what was formerly a luxury becomes standard, the need for basic financial education increases. How much do you know about budgets, your health care coverage, or even your retirement plan?

Too many fixed expenses. The rule is easy: If you owe more than your income, you are in trouble. Without a financial plan, you will not know how much you earn or how much you owe. You will look at your check each pay period and think you are "rich." With that feeling, you take on new debt, until you suddenly discover that you owe more than you earn. When you total all your debt (excluding a home mortgage), if it totals more than 10 percent of your annual income if you have one income, 15 percent if two incomes (wife and husband), or 20 percent if you have two incomes and you have three months' income in reserve (emergency funds), you have too much debt.

Failure to plan for emergencies. There is a common fear that "if I plan for an emergency, I am inviting it to happen." In truth, Murphy's Law is real: "If something can go wrong, it will." No matter how well you plan, emergencies, or at least unplanned financial expenses, are guaranteed to happen. If you do not make any provision for emergencies and they happen, they have the potential of destroying you, your finances, and all you care about.

Overestimating income and underestimating expenses. Without a financial plan, it is easy to react to the advertising circular, the television commercial, or the pitch of the friendly salesperson. Just a little more, or one more payment, cannot hurt your budget, can it?

Impulse buying. Without a plan, when you see something that looks good, what is to keep you from purchasing it?

Failure to communicate. Part of Bob's problem was that he and Darlene never talked about their financial situation. She was not aware that Bob could not pay all the bills. She spent as if everything were all right.

Failure to say no to children. I have seen more financial plans lead to panic situations because "we want the best for our children." Children will ask, and we will want to give them all they want. But when they know the financial limits, creative solutions can come from painful situations.

Failure to keep records. Records of what you spend and how much you earn are essential to controlling any financial plan. Records of what you have earned and spent will allow you to be prepared for whatever comes up. With records you will discover that there are really very few surprises. As a bonus, good records will help reduce your taxes.

Getting Out of Debt

Be a winner with planning! You can control your debt load if you want. The first step is commitment. Decide that you are going to take control of your spending and your charging. With a serious commitment to change and a plan to allow that change to happen, you have taken your first step to being a winner over your enemy—debt overload.

Bob broke down and cried when he explained the situation to Darlene. He was so afraid that she would think of him as a failure in their finances. "I didn't know," Darlene told Bob. "Let's figure out what we owe and design a plan to pay it off." Darlene was more understanding about the situation than Bob imagined. "I thought we had been spending a lot lately," Darlene explained to Bob, "but I thought you would say something to me if it were out of hand." The following steps are what Darlene and Bob implemented to get their debt under control and their bills all paid in fourteen months.

Control the plastic. Resolve not to charge anything else until your current credit cards are paid in full. Darlene and Bob emptied their wallets of all credit cards. They discovered that they had nine credit cards between them. They put all but one card each in their safety-deposit box at the bank. They reasoned that the harder it was to get the cards, the less they would use them. They kept one card each to aid in cashing checks down at the food store. But they promised each other not to charge anything on them. As their credit cards expired, they canceled the ones with the highest annual fee and the highest interest.

When their accounts were paid in full, they resolved only to charge those things they could pay in full when the statement came the next month. In an emergency, they reasoned, they would redesign their spending plan to pay off any debt within three months.

Understand the situation. Make a list of your debt. Without an overall picture of what you owe, it is easy to keep on charging. List who you owe, the balance of your debt, the interest on each debt, and the minimum payment due each month.

EXAMPLE

Item Due	Balance Owed	Interest	Minimum
First Bank	1,809.31	21.5%	$ 50.25
Second Bank	1,202.77	16.3%	35.35
Hardware	391.02	18.9%	20.00
Gas Card	177.30	13.2%	25.00
Department Store	494.90	18.9%	25.00
Department Store	935.83	21.5%	35.97
School Loan	4,349.17	7.75%	75.00
Auto Loan	8,940.75	9.9%	369.00
Auto Loan	2,417.40	13.5%	163.00

Understand your goals. Without clear financial goals, you will never make any plan work for long. Without any place to go, you will wander on your financial journey and get nowhere. Darlene and Bob's first goal was to pay off all their debt within eighteen months. In addition, they wanted to establish an emergency fund so that they would never be caught in such a bind again. They knew it would not be easy. They would have to change their lifestyle drastically in order to accomplish their goals. But they also knew that if they kept to their plan, everything would be paid in full in eighteen months. Actually, because of their plan, they paid it off four months early.

What goals do you have regarding your debts?

Win the budget battle. What resources do you have available in your spending plan? If you have a spending plan, you can review it before you make a purchase. "Do we have the money?" is a real question. Have we committed our resources to other areas of our spending plan? When in our spending plan can we make adjustments? There is only so much money. You cannot keep spending if the money is not there. Winning the budget battle (spending plan) will help you in your spending decisions.

Develop a plan. It is easier to limit your spending when you see the end. When you have a workable plan to pay off your debt in eighteen months, you can accept changes in your lifestyle because you know it will not last forever.

1. How much of your spending plan can you allocate to debt reduction? You may have to make some changes in your spending plan to allow more money to go to debt reduction.

2. Review your debt situation. Look at the complete picture. Allocate monthly payment to each debt. Pay off the debt with the higher interest first. If your credit card charges 21.5% interest and your school loan is only 7.75%, pay the minimum on your school loan and more on your credit cards.

3. Except for your home mortgage, auto loans, and perhaps your school loan, pay off all your debt within eighteen months. If that is impossible, do not extend your payment beyond thirty months. The longer you take, the more interest you will pay. The longer you take, the harder it is for you to see the end. (Note: Auto loans should not be longer than thirty-six months. Any longer and you will pay too much in interest for the value of the vehicle.)

4. Do not skip a payment. If you cannot make a payment, keep your creditors informed. Pay something on your balance. A creditor would rather work with you in scheduling a repayment plan than not be paid at all. Also beware of favors that credit companies want to give you. You will get letters from your creditors allowing you to skip a payment twice a year (usually in July and December). Remember, even if you skip a payment you will still be charged interest on your balance.

Also beware of unsolicited gifts in the mail. Last spring I received a check in the mail for $2,500. Because of my "superior credit" this finance company was going to give me the use of this money for twenty-four months. It was tempting. Then I figured the interest to be 34 percent a year. I quickly tore up the check and tossed it in the wastebasket.

5. Any time you have additional income, a bonus, IRS tax refund, or a gift, apply it to the balance of your debts.

6. As one debt balance is paid, add that payment to another debt. Your spending plan has already allocated that amount to debt reduction. If you reallocate that amount to your spending plan, it will just be absorbed. If you allocate it to your debt reduction plan, you will be free from debt faster than you planned.

7. When all your debt is paid, make a payment to yourself. If you will continue to make the same payment you made for debt reduction to your savings, you will be further along in all of your plans.

Celebrate your success. Make room in your plan to celebrate your accomplishments. Finding something to celebrate, such as paying off the balance of one loan, will make the entire process much easier. Be careful, however, not to charge your celebration to one of your other debts.

Control your spending. Your problem with debt is the result of your spending habits. Change your spending habits and you will eventually solve your problem. If you continue your lifestyle and spending habits, you will never be free of debt overload.

Bumper Snickers

How can I soar like an eagle,
when I keep spending like a turkey?

I owe, I owe, it's off to work I go!

Be a Smart Spender

Tolstoy tells the story of a man who would own all that he could encompass in a day's walk. Early one morning, as the sun came over the horizon, he began his journey. He began walking north. He took long but leisurely steps. He had figured his pace carefully and knew that at certain times he would have to turn. When it came time for his turn east, he thought he would go a little further north instead. By quickening his pace a little, he figured he could make up the time. Each time he turned, east, south, then west, he went a little further and walked a little faster. He was encompassing a lot of land.

During his walk, he had time to make elaborate plans on how he would use the land he would own to create great wealth. As the sun was beginning to set, he could be seen coming over the last hill. He was running for all he was worth. He had to make his starting point by sunset to claim the land. Just as the sun set, he ran to the point of his beginning. He'd won! Or had he? As he came to the point where he had begun his journey, the crowds gathered around him as he fell to the ground in exhaustion and died. He won it all but could have none of it.

If you have only limited financial resources, how much is enough? If your financial situation is bordering on overload, at some point you will have to answer that question. Changing your spending habits is a good place to start. If you continue spending as you have been, you will never get away from your enemy—debt. The following are some ways to change your spending habits.

Do not charge perishables. Perishables are those things that are gone or used up by the time the statement arrives. How easy it is to charge the vacation because the money is not available. You rationalize that you, your spouse, or the family as a whole, need the time away. Then when the bills begin arriving and there is not money to pay for the fun, you wonder why you did it. The same is true about Christmas gifts, a loaf of bread and a gallon of milk at the convenience store, or gas for your car.

Ask for a cash discount. Retailers pay credit card companies 3-5 percent of the purchase price for the privilege of charging. Ask retailers if they will give you a discount if you pay cash. After all, the retailer will get the sale and the money for it right away.

Do not buy impulsively. Do not get caught up in the emotion of the moment. Buy from your mind not from your heart. It is easy to be swayed by the sales pitch, the beauty of a particular item, or the day you have just had. Make it a policy to wait a week before any major purchase. At least hold off for two days before making a decision to buy that thing "you just have to have." In the meantime, think of something else. If you spend all your time thinking about this new thing, you will talk yourself into buying it. There

85

have been many times when I rationalized a purchase, only later to regret I ever talked myself into it.

Check your motives. Make it a habit before any major purchase to ask yourself the following questions:

> Do I need it?
> Have I done my research?
> Is the price reasonable?
> Is this really a sale price?
> Can I substitute something else for it?
> Will it solve my inner need?

Shop with a list. Go with a list and buy only what is on your list. If you go grocery shopping when you are hungry, everything looks good. If you just browse around in a department store, you will find something that you could use, someday.

Be a careful shopper. Do you clip coupons? Sometimes they are a real savings. Sometimes even with the discount the item is more expensive than a good substitute. Know your products and know their prices. Do you buy prepackaged food? You are paying for the privilege of letting someone do the work for you. Prepare your own meals for better and less expensive meals.

Buy quality. The purchase of a less expensive item, such as a couch, may cost you more because it will wear out faster. Check the quality as well as the price. If what you want costs more, wait two or three months while you save up for the difference.

Rent occasionally used items. Do you have a garage full of tools or a sewing machine you only use once a year? Those items are best rented for the time you need them and then returned. That way you have up-to-date, well-maintained tools, with no capital outlay.

Beware of rent-to-own. There is a time to rent, and there is a time to buy. Do not get confused between the two. A rent-to-own product is simply installment buying, often at a higher purchase price. If you have to purchase something on installment, then you are not ready to buy that product. Either purchase an equal item at less cost (i.e., a 21″ television rather than a 27″), or save until you can purchase what you want.

Settle for less. When you eat out, order hamburger instead of steak. Better yet, invite someone over to your house for a barbecue.

List your own. List ten additional ways you can reduce your spending:

1.

2.

3.

4.

5.

6.

7.

8.

9.

10.

When all is said and done, there are only three ways to deal with debt overload: cut your spending, increase your income, reduce your standard of living.

If nothing else works for you, don't hesitate to get help. In most states, and in many metropolitan communities, there is a Consumer Credit Counseling Center. For little or no fee, they will help you design a repayment plan and keep you out of bankruptcy court. To find the office nearest you, check your Yellow Pages, or send a stamped, self-addressed envelope to: National Foundation for Consumer Credit, 8701 Georgia Avenue, Suite 507, Silver Spring, MD 30910.

> When we like ourselves
> we are less likely to use
> external things to fill
> the emptiness.
>
> Jane Brody

Chapter Six
ESTATE PLANNING AND THE CHRISTIAN

> *Our sense of self depends heavily on what we possess. We are in a very real way extensions of the things we have.*
>
> Russell W. Belk

> *When we cry, "Abba! Father!" it is that very Spirit bearing witness with our spirit that we are children of God, and if children, then heirs, heirs of God and joint heirs with Christ.*
>
> (Romans 8:15-17)

Why do we postpone doing the important things in life until it is too late? Sam and Marie were in their middle thirties. They both had good jobs. Sam was a high school mathematics teacher and coach, and Marie was a CPA. They had a beautiful house on the outskirts of town. Sally and John, their young children, were a bundle of energy but good children. One night Sam and Marie were on their way home from church when something happened. Their car went off the road. They were discovered two hours later, but it was too late.

Sam and Marie thought that retirement and estate planning were for older persons. Without an estate plan, and especially without a will, their estate, including the two children, was turned over to a probate court. Their families fought over who would take care of the children. That fight, the paying of accumulated debts, court costs, and attorney's fees used up most of what Sam and Marie left as an estate.

Contrary to popular opinion, *estate planning is for the living*. It is a portrait of who you are. It is an expression of your love for your family and friends. It is a declaration of how you see yourself in relationship with God.

In chapter one we expressed our relationship with God as that of a steward. The steward exclaims in voice and in action that all he or she has in life belongs to God. We possess what we have because of God's trust in us. What we have is ours to use in an intimate relationship with God. Together with God, our partner, we will strive to achieve in this world God's kingdom.

Does our relationship as steward end with our death? I don't think so! In fact, as Christians we affirm that by Jesus' action on the cross, we are victorious over death. The concept of eternity with God is not just a hopeful promise. It is fact! Paul declares it most boldly in 1 Corinthians 15. Jesus' resurrection is the first step for all. "Thanks be to God, who gives us the victory through our Lord Jesus Christ" (1 Cor. 15:57).

If it is true that six to eight of every ten people who die yearly do not have a valid will, then estate planning is both a societal and a Christian concern. As a Christian steward I have tried to manage God's assets in a way consistent with God's will. If everything is God's, and in my partnership with God I have accumulated an estate, isn't that God's, too? If I try to be a good Christian steward in my "living years," how can I ignore that concern at my death?

Estate planning is another step in my partnership with God. It is a plan to continue that partnership by transferring assets, either now or at my death. It is a decision to continue God's plan through me, in a way that also minimizes tax liability.

As estate plan is for the living. By the time of your death it is too late to work on your estate plan. In preparing your estate plan, ask yourself, "By what do I want to be remembered?" Will you be remembered for your love of family and friends, for your acts of generosity, and by your faithful witness to God? Or, will you be remembered by your lack of planning which left your family destitute while your estate was tied up in the probate courts?

Why is the establishment of an estate plan avoided by so many? The following are excuses I have heard for avoiding the simple step of establishing a will. Which of these are true about you?

Death. "I am afraid that if I initiate a will, I will die." All of us will die sooner or later. Some of us believe that any talk of death will make it sooner. I asked an attorney who specializes in estate planning if any of his clients died within a week of signing their will. There were none he could name.

Cost. It is true that every good estate plan needs the help of an attorney at some point in the process. For those who have never used the services of an attorney, there is an unfounded fear that it "costs too much." In fact, a simple will may cost as little as $75 to $100. That will may save your estate thousands of dollars in settlement costs when you die.

Lack of information. When we don't know much about a subject, we assume it is more complex than it really is. Because we do not know about estate planning, we avoid the subject. This chapter is designed to provide you with information written in simple, lay (nonlegal) language.

89

No attorney. The issue I hear from many people is that they do not have an attorney and do not know how to select one. The best way to begin is to ask your pastor. Pastors know people in the community, hear what others say, and are aware of attorneys who are members of your church. As a last resort, check the Yellow Pages or call the Bar Association in your area. Better yet, ask your friends whom they have used. Do not hesitate to ask if there is a charge for the initial session and/or what the fees are. Most attorneys have indicated to me that they do not charge for their first meeting with a client. Select an attorney in your area and meet with him or her to see what you need to do.

Estate too small. The reason many of us do not worry about an estate plan is that we assume that our estate is too small. No estate is too small. If you care about your family and friends, if your faith is important to you, then you need an estate plan. In fact, you were probably surprised when you compiled your statement of net worth in chapter three. Most of us are surprised to find our net worth is more than we anticipated.

Singleness. A friend of mine said to me the other day, "I'm single, so why do I need an estate plan?" Whether you are single, married, or single-again is not the issue. What do you want to happen with what you leave behind? Bobby suffered a debilitating stroke about a year after his wife died. He couldn't talk. He couldn't move. He couldn't do anything for himself. But because his estate plan included a durable power of attorney, his best friend John could take care of Bobby and his business as if Bobby were making those decisions himself.

Age. "I'm still young. I have a long time to go before I need to worry about that." Death and disability do not respect age. Remember Sam and Marie? If you have young children, guardianship is a critical issue *now.*

Tomorrow. The best laid plans dissolve into yesterdays because tomorrows never come. The only way you will do anything about your estate plan is to resolve to do something now. Finish this chapter. Complete the inventory and make an appointment to see your attorney.

I resolve to:

1. Complete my estate planning inventory by _____.

2. Make an appointment with an attorney by _____.

Everyone Has an Estate Plan

"What happens if I don't do anything?" Let's be clear, everyone has an estate plan. Either you design your own or the state, through its probate process, will do it for you. If you do not care, the state does.

What is probate? Probate is the process by which the state, through its legal (court) system, validates your last will and testament. In the absence of a will, the probate court takes control of your estate. The probate court will take charge of your assets, pay all taxes and other expenses, and distribute the remainder of your assets according to a formula established by your state legislature. If you have minor children, the state will decide their guardianship and care. The courts will designate a trustee to care for your estate, decide what is best for your children, and pay for their expenses until the courts decide they can care for themselves. This is not done for nothing. Expenses for the management of your estate will have to be paid from the assets in your estate.

Nine Estate Planning Sins

Being your own attorney. There is a real temptation to avoid an attorney and write your own will. There are will packets advertised on television and in magazines where you fill in the blanks. There are computer programs which will organize your thoughts. But there is no substitute for an attorney. A friend told me a story about his mother. Using a kit, she wrote her own will. She even got two witnesses. But she forgot to sign it herself. She didn't have a large estate, but it was in probate court for nearly two years. The result was far from what she intended.

Letting the state decide your wishes. Failure to do anything will invite the state to decide for you. Without a will, estate administration costs will increase, family arguments (among themselves and the state) will grow, and the estate God and you built will not be what you expected. In addition, no probate process makes provision for charitable giving.

Family security. Without an estate plan, your family may not be prepared for the economic upheaval of your death. Have you made provision through insurance or other planning tools to provide income for your family when you are gone? Each adult in a family provides a significant economic benefit to that home. Whether an income earner or a provider of services, when one of those persons is gone, who will care for that economic benefit?

Guardianship. Without a will, and without a provision in your will to care for your children, what will happen to them when you die? We all think, "If I die, my spouse will be here to care for the children." What happens when you both die, like Sam and Marie? Who do you want to care for your children? What will happen to your estate? Young children cannot manage it.

91

Have you made a provision for a trust to manage your assets and care for your children until they are of age?

Failure to protect heirs from themselves. A well-thought-out estate plan will ease the strain on the family. Are your family members equipped to receive and manage what you leave behind? Is an eighteen-year-old, or a twenty-five-year-old, or even a thirty-five-year-old equipped to receive a large inheritance? Will all your estate be "flittered away" in no time at all? Dwight and Joan, in chapter two, lost their inheritance through taxes and mismanagement. If Joan's parents had left their estate in a trust, Joan and Dwight might have had a better life.

Liquidity. Is your estate tied up in property or other illiquid assets? Will your estate be forced to sell when the market value is low? Have you made provisions, through insurance or other plans, to fund your estate until your assets can be distributed?

Inadequate administrator. Have you chosen someone who is familiar with you and the way you operate to administer your estate at your death? I have seen family members struggle with an estate they were ill-equipped to manage. Does your administrator know where to find all your important documents?

No charitable gift. Have you made a provision in your estate plan to make a charitable gift? Have you included your church in your will? Your church and other charities you support will lose not only your presence but your financial support when you die. If they are important to you now, can you make a gift that will keep on giving? A gift from your estate to your church or favorite charity's endowment program will allow you to support that ministry forever.

Too much tax. The federal government has an estate tax of up to 55 percent. Most states have either an estate or inheritance tax. Even if you think your estate is relatively small, it may be subject to one of these taxes. A well-planned estate, and a charitable gift from your estate, will lessen the possibility of those taxes. After all, who wants to pay more tax than is necessary?

Ingredients of a Faithful Estate Plan

So you are convinced! You need an estate plan. Where do you begin? What do you need to know and how do you design an estate plan? Before you go to an attorney, you need to think through a number of issues. Begin by asking what you want to happen to your estate, your family, your friends, and your favorite charity when you die, and make plans to accomplish those objectives. A faithful estate plan has at least three objectives. These objectives are summarized in these three most asked questions:

What will happen to my estate when I die?

How can I minimize estate and inheritance taxes?

How can I make a charitable contribution through my estate?

Your estate is composed of not only your assets but people as well. We do not like to think about our death, but to postpone planning for it has great consequences. In financial planning we ask ourselves, "What do we want to accomplish in our financial plan?" In estate planning we ask, "What and who is important?"

As you begin to design an estate plan, what is important to you?

Who are the people most important to you? List those persons you would want to remember in your estate plan and their relationship to you.

Reread the list of persons you want to remember. How would you want to remember them?

Every estate plan needs someone who will carry out your plans. That person is called by a variety of names: administrator, executor, or personal representative. You will want a person who thinks like you, can administer your estate, and has the best interest in caring for those you leave behind.

What qualities are important to you in choosing an administrator of your estate?

Name three persons (or positions: e.g., attorney, CPA) you know who best fit your needs for an administrator. Rank them in order of your preference.

If you have children under the age of eighteen, you will want to name a guardian for them. A guardian is a person (or persons) you feel would best carry on your interests in raising your children. If you could choose someone to raise your children, what qualities would you look for in such a person?

Who do you know that best fulfills that description? Are they willing and able to accept such a responsibility? Have you provided adequate resources for them to manage your estate?

Organizations as well as individuals play an important part in your life. Which charities, church, or organizations are important to you? How would you like to remember these organizations in your plan?

What you own still exists after your death. Except for the Pharaohs of ancient Egypt and the woman who was buried in her Cadillac, you cannot take it with you. Imagine that you are your own administrator. What is to be included in your estate? How will your administrator locate all your assets and important papers?

Make an inventory of all you possess. Make a complete list. Go over it several times. List policies and account numbers. List the location of all important papers, contracts, and accounts. The following inventory list will help you gather this information.

Estate Planning Inventory

Date of Inventory

Names/Birth dates/Social Security
  numbers
  Husband
  Wife
  Dependents

Wedding date
Previous marriage information

Family Tree

Will Information
  Attorney—Name/Address/Phone
  Location of will
  Administrator of estate—Name/
    Address/Phone
  Persons to notify at time of death—
    Name/Address/Phone

Living Will
  Location

Key Advisors: Name/Address/Phone/
  Account numbers
  Attorney
  Accountant
  Banker
  Broker
  Insurance agents
  Pastor
  Physician
  Trust officer
  Other

Location of Important Papers
  Social Security numbers
  Certificates
    Birth
    Marriage
    Other
  Military history
    Branch of service
    Dates

Copy of discharge papers

Employment record
Organizations in which you are active
Education
Funeral and burial
  Location of burial lots
Funeral instructions
Property
  Personal
  Business
Mortgages
  Personal
  Business

Financial Records: record location and
  account numbers

  Bank accounts
  Certificates of deposit
  U.S. savings bonds
  Stocks and bonds
  Mutual funds
  Property
  Pension accounts
  IRAs
  Insurance
    Disability
    Life
    Auto
    Home
    Health
  Credit cards
  Tax records

Personal Property Inventory
  Automobiles
  Jewelry
  Boats
  Object of art
  Other valuable personal property

Date _____

Signed _____

This inventory tells a story; it paints a picture and will open your eyes to who you are. It is a valuable tool for both your estate and financial plans. Update this inventory each year. Put a copy in your safety-deposit box, in the files of your estate administrator, and keep one for your own use.

Estate Planning Tools

Paying as little as possible in estate taxes is a goal for everyone I know. Actually, the United States has a very generous estate tax plan. Estate tax is a federal tax on the transfer of property at a person's death. Each person is exempt from the Federal Estate Tax for an estate up to $600,000. An estate beyond this amount is taxed at a rate of 37-55 percent.

There are ways, during life and at death, to transfer assets from one's estate beyond this $600,000 exemption and still avoid the estate tax. Any person, during one's life or at death, may transfer an unlimited amount to his or her spouse and not be subject to an estate or gift tax. In addition, an individual may give any number of persons up to $10,000 a year (or $20,000 in a joint gift) without incurring an estate or gift tax.

The most basic estate planning tool is a will. Everyone needs a will. Each individual adult needs a will. Husbands and wives need separate wills. A will, when properly written, is a legal document which can, at your death:

> Name your estate administrator.
> Name a guardian for your minor children.
> Transfer ownership of property.
> Make gifts to individuals and charities.
> Establish trusts.

With the help of an attorney, write your will to reflect your wishes today. With every major change in your life (divorce, death of a spouse, remarriage, moving, retirement, etc.), you will want to reevaluate the provisions in your will. This, too, needs to be done with an attorney. Writing on your will may invalidate the entire will.

In addition to your will, you will want to leave a letter of instruction. This is a letter to your estate administrator. This should be a separate document from your will. This is only to guide your administrator; it is not a legal document. Since it is easier to make changes to this letter than a will, you can use this to detail your wishes. This letter may be a statement about your funeral and how it is to be handled. You may want to detail how certain items are to go to certain people. It may be a letter to all you leave behind. Go over this letter and your will with your estate administrator.

In addition to the will, more and more people are adding a trust to their estate plan. Like a will, a trust is a legal document drawn up by an attorney. A trust is an agreement whereby an individual transfers ownership of property to the trust to manage for the benefit of him/herself or another. A trust can go into effect either while the creator of the trust is alive (inter-vivos) or by his/her will (testamentary) at the time of death. A trust can be either revocable (the ability to change or dissolve the trust) or irrevocable (nonchanging).

98

The trust is fast becoming as standard a tool in estate planning as the will. The trust document is a valuable tool used to manage your estate when you are no longer able to do so by disability or death. If there were a time when either you, your spouse, a child, or someone to whom you would leave your estate could no longer manage the estate, the trust could do it for you.

You may have a child or parent for whom you feel responsible. But you do not want to burden that person with the management of an estate. You may want to ensure his/her care beyond your death. You can establish a trust to care for that person and then at his/her death the remainder of the trust could be transferred to another person or charity.

In these days of divorce, remarriage, and blended families, a trust is a valuable tool to ensure the care of a spouse and yet the ultimate transfer of an estate to one's children.

Life insurance has long been an estate-planning tool. It is a way to fund your estate with immediate money to pay for your last illness and funeral expenses. It is a way to provide an income for those who rely on your earning power until they are on their own. It is also a way to make a gift to your favorite charity.

A valuable estate-planning tool that is not known by many is the "power of attorney." The power of attorney, and especially a durable power of attorney, is a transfer of your rights to decide to another. This is especially important if something happens to you and you are not able to decide for yourself. Being comatose or being a victim of Alzheimer's disease are just two examples of times when you could not act for yourself.

Along with the durable power of attorney, the "living will" is an essential estate-planning tool. Remember earlier when I wrote that "an estate plan is for the living"? Everyone dreads the possibility of a long and lingering death. What would you want done if your recovery were without hope, yet you were kept alive by machine? A living will is a legal document, again prepared by an attorney, by which you designate someone else to make decisions for you if you are unable to do so. This is not a complete listing of estate-planning possibilities. To complete your estate plan, you need the benefit of an attorney.

Charitable Giving through Your Estate

Because of what God has done in Jesus Christ, and because of your relationship with a church or charity, you may want to make charitable giving part of your estate plan. You can make a gift from your estate now, while you are alive, or at your death. You can make a gift now, continue to receive income until your death, and still make a sizable charitable contribution.

As a young pastor, I knew a woman who had very little. She had no immediate family. Her husband had died some years before. But she loved the church and wanted to give something to the church. She was already giving more than I thought she could. All I knew about giving was giving outright cash. That which she had available, she needed for everyday living. We were stuck! Then the director of our conference's foundation came to our church to give a seminar. There she and I discovered there were other options for giving. She discovered that she could give her house to the church and still live in it all her life. When she died, the church could sell her house and use the proceeds for the youth ministries of the church (her pet concern).

There are many options for giving and many ways of giving. Almost anything which has a value and can be converted into cash may be a suitable option for charitable giving. Some people may want to give something for which the church can receive an immediate benefit (current). Still others, because of financial constraints or personal commitment, may want to give something now but use it until they die (deferred), after which the church can benefit.

The following summary is a partial list of charitable giving options. For further information on each subject read the appropriate description which follows:

Current	*Deferred*
Cash	Bequests
Appreciated securities	Life insurance policies
Tangible personal property	IRAs or other retirement plans
Appreciated real estate	Revocable living trusts
Cash value life insurance	Life estate agreements
Money market, certificates of deposit, passbook accounts	Charitable remainder trusts
Lead trusts	Life income arrangements

1. Giving Cash

Giving cash is the first thought most people have when they think about giving. Persons giving cash may actually give a smaller gift than they really wanted to give because of the limits on their available reserves. Not only may it not be the most appropriate gift at the time, it may actually cost less to give the same amount (or a larger amount) by giving something other than cash.

You want to give $10,000 right now to a special missions project through your church. You have the money in a money market account and can write a check. Of course you will need to sell some of your XYZ stock to replenish your money market account.

100

If you sold the stock this is what might happen:

$10,000 Fair market value of stock if sold
$ 1,000 Basis (what was paid for the stock)
$ 9,000 Taxable capital gain
$ 2,520 Capital gains tax (if at 28 percent tax bracket)
$ 7,480 After-tax balance

In this example, after selling the stock, you have only $7,480.00 after taxes to replenish your money market account. On the other hand, if you gave the church the stock worth $10,000 you might avoid the tax consequence altogether (as would the church).

Other giving options may also provide better giving possibilities. Let us examine the ones used most often in charitable giving.

2. Giving through Your Will

The easiest way for you to make a charitable gift may well be through your will. You have probably never thought of including the church in your estate plan. No one in the church may have mentioned that as a possibility.

Statistics around the country show that between 65 percent and 85 percent of those who die each year die without a valid will. If there is no valid will, the probate courts will decide the disposition of one's estate. No state includes charitable giving in its plans.

There are several ways to include charitable giving through your will:

A. A *fixed amount* can be placed in a will: "I want to give $5,000 to XYZ United Church." Although most common, this may not be the best way to include the church. Designating an amount does not have any relation to faith desires, to your entire estate, nor does it grow with inflation as does the remainder of the estate.

B. *A specific item* such as a rare painting, a home, or a piece of property adjoining the church can be transferred through the use of a will.

C. Better than a specific dollar amount, you can designate a *percentage of your estate* to be given to the church. If a tithe is the standard of giving for Christians, then including 10 percent of your estate would be one appropriate suggestion. The bequest then grows in the same proportion as the entire estate, thus fulfilling the wishes of the benefactor.

D. Most estates are larger than the individual realizes. After all other bequests are granted, you could give all that is left *(residual)* to the church. You could give an amount, specific property, or percentage to

101

the church, fulfill other bequests as well, and then grant the residual to the church.

3. Giving Appreciated Securities

The gift of securities held more than a year may avoid capital gains tax and secure a sizable charitable tax deduction at the same time. There are many people who have appreciated securities, with minimal dividends, that they cannot afford to sell because of the capital gains consequences. Contributing such securities to a church may allow you to satisfy a giving goal, while other resources can be used to satisfy investment goals. (See the example under "Giving Cash" for a description of this form of giving.)

4. Giving Real Estate

Real estate, especially the family home, is often the largest asset in one's estate. You may think you have nothing to give because all you have is property. But giving property may be both an answer to your giving plans and a solution to your estate planning goals. You may give property (personal, rental, and business property) outright, as a life estate, or in a bargain sale.

Giving property outright, without any strings, is the easiest and most common of the ways of giving property. While someone is alive, or through a will, property can be transferred to the church without any major complications. The property should be free of any legal claims (i.e., delinquent taxes, mortgage, or liens).

If you own property, want to make a gift of that property while you are still alive, yet still need the use of that property, there is a plan for you, too. It is called a "life-estate." In this form of giving, the donor and the church enter into a legal agreement called a life-estate agreement. Title to the property is transferred to the church and registered by the County Clerk responsible for handling deeds. The property is now owned by the church, but the donor retains life use of the property. When the donor dies, the church takes possession of the property and uses it, or the proceeds from its sale, according to the wishes of the donor.

In a few cases, persons may want the church to have their property, but they really need some of the equity out of the property for their own care and upkeep. The solution, in this case, may well be what is called a "bargain sale." A bargain sale is accomplished when appreciated assets (usually, but not always, real estate) are gifted in part and sold in part to the charity.

5. Giving Personal Property

Almost anything of value that can be readily sold or turned into cash can be gifted to the church. Such gifts often include, but are not limited to, art objects, antiques, coin and stamp collections, cars, and even boats. The list of items of personal property that can be gifted to the church is limited only by a donor's estate.

6. Giving through Life Insurance

There are many ways of using life insurance in making a charitable gift. Some ways require no additional outlay of capital on the part of the donor; some require only modest payments which result in relatively substantial gifts; and some provide tax relief for capital gains.

One option for giving with insurance is to use a paid-up policy which is no longer needed (i.e., your family is raised). There are many policies in existence today which have been "forgotten" by the owner and beneficiary. Even when these policies are of a low face amount, they can benefit the designated charitable beneficiary at the time of the insured's death. If the charity is made both the owner and the beneficiary of the policy, the donor may take a deduction of the replacement value of the policy on income taxes immediately.

If there is an existing policy on which policy premiums are still being made but which is no longer needed, this policy can be given to the church. When the church is made the owner and beneficiary of the policy, the donor can make contributions to the church to continue paying the policy. In this example, the continued payment and an amount equal to the cash surrender value of the policy can be deducted as a charitable contribution.

Another option is to purchase a new policy for the purpose of making a gift. This type of giving is often a good alternative to guarantee commitments to a capital campaign should the donor die prior to the completion of her/his commitments.

Insurance is also used to replace an asset given to charity. You may want to make a gift of property to your church today but do not want to deplete your estate for your children or other heirs. In this situation, insurance may be purchased to replace the gifted property.

For persons who wish to give the church a life insurance gift but also want to keep part of the value of the insurance in their estate, a partial gift of insurance is possible.

7. Giving through Life Income Arrangement

There are times when persons of faith want to make a charitable gift but also feel that they need to increase their annual income. They are in a quandary. Is there anything they can do? The charitable gift annuity is becoming the most popular answer to this problem.

The charitable gift annuity is an exchange of something of value (usually cash, appreciated property, or appreciated securities) for the guarantee of an income for life. The charity guarantees an income for life (usually through a life insurance company). On the death of the income beneficiary (and/or his/ her survivor), the remainder of the asset goes to charity (the church). The amount of the periodic payment is set by government tables according to the beneficiary's life expectancy.

8. Giving through Trust Agreements

Most people know about wills and think that the will is the only way to make a gift when they die. A trust may be used during one's life to transfer assets yet retain control and use of those assets until death. At death, those assets may be transferred according to the donor's wishes, without going through the probate (court) process.

Although there are various ways to use a trust, the most common uses for giving include:

A. *Charitable Remainder Trust*—In this arrangement, property is transferred to a trust, with the remainder interest given to a qualified charity. The donor has the use of the property, with all income generated by the property, during the donor's life or for a period of time. At death, the remaining value of the trust is transferred to charity according to the donor's wishes.

B. *Charitable Lead Trust*—This arrangement is just the opposite of the charitable remainder trust. With the use of a charitable lead trust, the charity has the use of the property or the income generated by the trust for a period of years. At the end of the trust term, the property is returned to the donor or the beneficiary as described in the trust arrangement.

9. Giving through IRA or Other Retirement Plan

Most people do not realize they can include a charity as a beneficiary on their IRA, profit-sharing plan, Keogh, tax-sheltered annuity, or company pension plan. Gifts through these arrangements come from the remainder in the plans at the death of the donor and/or beneficiary.

A person may advise the retirement plan administrator to name the church as a beneficiary of the plan. This may be done in one of many ways. At the death of the donor before retirement, the church can be named to receive:

104

A. *Part or all of the remainder* in the plan.

B. *As secondary beneficiary of the remainder* in the plan, only after the death of the donor and the primary beneficiary (e.g., spouse).

C. *As the last beneficiary of the remainder* in the plan, only after the death of the donor, the primary beneficiary (e.g., spouse), and other beneficiaries (e.g., children). In this case there may be no gift to the church. But in the event all beneficiaries die while there is a remainder in the plan, the church would be the beneficiary of this residual.

At the death of the donor after retirement begins, the church may be named to receive:

A. *Part or all of the remainder in the plan when the donor dies.*

B. *Part or all of the remainder at the death of the primary beneficiary.*

C. *Part or all of the remainder following the death of the primary and secondary beneficiaries.*

10. Giving Cash Equivalents

When cash is not an option, a person may want to place the church's name as the second (joint) name on bank accounts: checking and savings accounts, money market accounts, certificates of deposit, as well as other cash equivalent accounts. During his or her life, the donor has the full use of value in, and income from, these accounts. Donors can cash in and/or use these accounts as they wish. At the donor's death, the remainder in these accounts would be transferred to the church.

Special Notes

1. Many of these options for giving need the benefit of expert assistance in the giving and management of assets and giving options (i.e., gift annuities). The regional foundation and/or office of development of your favorite charity can be of assistance in the counseling, securement, and management of these giving possibilities.

2. The summary is based on the law current at the time of publication. Illustrations showing benefits of charitable giving are solely for educational purposes. For information on current law and specific recommendations, each person should consult her or his own qualified professional advisor.

CHAPTER SEVEN
LIFE PLANNING

> *For surely I know the plans I have for you, says the Lord, plans for your welfare and not for harm, to give you a future with hope* (Jeremiah 29:11).
>
> *Be doers of the word, and not merely hearers who deceive themselves* (James 1:22).
>
> *What good is it . . . if you say you have faith but do not have works?* (James 2:14).

Throughout this book we have been identifying the different steps in financial planning. Financial planning was defined as identifying one's goals, recognizing one's assets, and coordinating the two. Christian financial planning is the application of one's Christian faith and values to that financial plan.

Carmen was forty-two when she decided she needed a financial plan. She was alone again, now that her son had left for college. She had done well raising Pedro by herself. Between her savings and his scholarship at Old State University, his four years in college were guaranteed. She had a good job down at Pfeifer and Pfeifer. She had an attractive pension plan, had invested in an IRA when that was possible, and had a few dollars in a mutual fund. Three weeks ago she revealed to her church school class, in response to a lesson on the Apostle Paul's missionary journey, that she always wanted to be a missionary. In order to do that in thirteen years, she needed a plan.

The hardest step in financial planning is putting it all together. We can read all we can get our hands on. We can become pseudo-accountants in designing record systems and keeping track of our spending plan. We can even carefully design an estate plan. But until we put it all together, our good intentions will disappear as quick as the lemon pie on the kitchen counter.

Can you picture a young girl slipping down a dark chute in Lewis Carroll's *Alice in Wonderland?* Knowing that she was lost, when Alice came upon that big cat she asked which way she should go. The wise cat answered, "That all depends on where you are going." Alice cried out, "I don't really care where, as long as I get somewhere." To which the cat answered, "Then it doesn't matter which way you go." If it doesn't matter to you where you are going, then most any way you go will get you somewhere. But if you have specific goals, like Carmen, then you need a plan.

The purpose of this chapter is to bring together all we identified in the previous chapters into some kind of accomplishable plan. It is an attempt to coordinate your goals, your resources, and your faith into a plan that works for you. Every plan is different. Your plan will not be like Betty's or Bob's. It is unique to you, your resources, and your response to God. That plan must be flexible. It will change and must be able to adapt to detours on your financial and life journey.

The purpose of a financial plan is to accomplish God's, and your, plan for your life. If one of your goals is to retire at age sixty-two and volunteer your time in the local thrift store, you cannot wait until you are age sixty and hope you are financially secure. God wants you to plan.

There will be peaks and valleys in your financial life. There will be times when your spending will be greater than your earnings. There will also be times when your earnings will be greater than your spending. One goal of financial planning is to even out those peaks and valleys in your income and expenditures.

Retirement is one of those valleys, when spending will be greater than income. Sending your children to college, receiving a bill for insurance, and sometimes an unexpected visit by your relatives may all be times when spending is greater than income. Unless a plan is created to cover the excess expenditures, you will be caught in a crisis. Unless a plan is created to save in times of excess income, any expenditure beyond the regular spending plan will create a crisis.

Spending is not always predictable as to amount, duration, or time. You may not know the precise cost or time that your daughter will need braces, the first payment is due at Old State University, or exactly when the car will need new tires. But you do know that all those things will happen, sometime. Surprises in you financial plan do not need to be crisis points, if you are ready. Some of those surprises are predictable. If you are ready for them, these surprises become only slight detours in your financial plan.

Some Assembly Required

When our sons were five and four years of age, we bought them an air hockey game for Christmas. I am not a mechanic. When I saw the words "some assembly required" stenciled on the side of the box, I did not give it a second thought. When the boys were securely in bed, Uncle Carl and I took the box out of its hiding place. When all the pieces of the game were scattered around the floor, I thought there was enough to build a car. "Some assembly" meant four hours of putting together, taking apart, reading the instructions, and finally getting it together. When the boys got up at 6:30

107

Christmas morning, they were excited. *I* was tired, having had only three hours of sleep.

Now it is your turn. You do not need to stay up until 3:00 in the morning. But if you are going to have a plan, you will need to put it together. The first step in assembling your life plan is to identify goals. In chapter three you began identifying goals. Turn back to that section to refresh your memory of the goals you identified.

The form "My Financial Plan" (p. 110) will help you gather information from previous chapters. The form is divided into four sections ranging from six months to more than five years. What I did with this form for my planning was to divide my life into four segments: (1) what I want to do within a year (now); (2) what I want to do until my boys are out of college (short-range); (3) the time from their being on their own until I retire (medium-range); and (4) my retirement years (long-term).

Use the form to schedule your plans. Your life may not fall as easily into four segments. There is nothing significant about four sections. You may be starting out with your financial plan at age twenty-two. Everything seems so far away and impossible to accomplish. Begin focusing on the immediate time frame.

Whatever your age or position in your financial plan, if you divide your plan into workable segments, you will find it more manageable. In too many plans we see only the big picture. We want to buy a house, get out of debt, put the kids through college, and have a secure retirement. When we look at all that and try to do it all at once, it seems impossible. But when we divide it into workable parts, it makes it easier to plan.

Larry and Diane were frustrated and a little scared with this process at first. They were in their late twenties and had two children, Rob and Sally. They listed their major goals as:

1. Buying a house in three years
2. Getting out of debt (except for the mortgage)
3. Tithing to their church
4. Putting the children through college
5. Being comfortable in retirement
6. Spending one week each year on a mission project
7. Having an emergency fund of $1,500

When Larry and Diane looked at their list, they thought it was impossible to do it all. But when they broke down their goals into workable segments it seemed possible.

They really wanted to buy a house. They were renting a house now and wanted to get into one of their own. But they also wanted to tithe. That seemed most important to them. They figured they were giving about 4 percent of their income to the church. Jumping from 4 percent to a tithe and

108

saving for a house seemed impossible. By increasing their giving by 1 percent a year, their goal of tithing became possible. In six years or less, they would be giving a full tithe. They saw a point in time when they could reach their goal.

Larry and Diane had $4,000 in a savings account for a house. They figured they needed $10,000 for a down payment, closing costs, and moving expenses. By reworking their spending plan and taking minimal vacations, they figured they could have enough for a down payment in three years. Diane literally jumped in the air.

Debt was not a major problem, they decided. But using credit cards really put a bite in their spending plan. They decided not to use their credit cards, except in an emergency. If it was not in their spending plan, or if they could not work it into their spending plan, they would not buy it. In addition, they would pay off their credit card debt in nine months.

Retirement income, other than Social Security and company pension plans, would have to wait until after they moved into their house. Waiting can be part of a plan, as long as there is a decision to do something at a specific point in time.

Their other goals were met with small steps as a beginning. The children's education fund and the emergency fund would each get $50 a month. Next year they would increase each fund to $100 a month. In three years they would reevaluate the education fund and begin a more intense savings plan.

Step One is to identify your goals, how much is needed for each goal, and which goals to work on first. Larry and Diane were able to get their plan into a workable design and it was fun.

Using the form "My Financial Plan," write down your goals. Identify goals you can accomplish in a short period of time. Seeing something accomplished makes long-term goals seem possible too. Figure a dollar amount for each goal. Larry and Diane needed $6,000 within three years, along with their $4,000 for a down payment on their dream house. Their financial need was to save $6,000 in three years.

My Financial Plan

Now: Six months to a year

Goal	Financial Need	Financial Plan

Short-term: One to three years

Goal	Financial Need	Financial Plan

Medium: Three to five years

Goal	Financial Need	Financial Plan

Long-term: More than five years

Goal	Financial Need	Financial Plan

Earlier in this book you wrote down some other objectives or goals (p. 44). Now is the time to retrieve them. Which faith goals have you set for yourself?

1.

2.

3.

From chapter five, did you make any goals regarding debt management that need to be included?

1.

2.

3.

Chapter six on estate planning invited you to make some goals regarding your estate. Which estate planning goals need to be included in your plan? How can these goals be integrated into your financial plan?

1.

2.

3.

Step Two is to discover how much you have available from your spending plan to spend on your goals. In chapter three you worked on your spending plan. How much can your spending plan allow for these "special objectives"? Where in your spending plan can you make changes in order to reallocate some current expense to these future goals?

In any plan some adjustments to lifestyle must happen in order for goals to be accomplished. If you are spending $100 a week at local restaurants, can you cut that back to $50 a week and apply that extra $50 toward your number one goal? Instead of taking a major vacation to the mountains or the beach every year, can you take a mini-vacation every other year and put the extra $2,500 into the children's education fund? Instead of a new car this year, how much will you save it you wait a year? What are three ways you can find extra income in your spending plan to allocate toward your goals?

1.

2.

3.

Let me add a note about some good news and bad news in financial planning. Although we will not look at the ways to invest in this book, there are several principles you must know to expand your financial base.

First the bad news. Inflation will cause almost everything to cost more in the future. If one year of college at Old State U. will cost $6,250 this year, with college costs increasing at 6 percent a year, it will cost $9,397.69 in eight years for one year of college. Without figuring the increased cost, our plan will fall short.

The good news is "compound interest." Money invested over a period of time will earn interest. If that interest is left in the account, it too will earn interest. In order to have enough money for that first year in college in eight years, you only need $4,716.38 invested today at 9 percent.

Another way of looking at what you need is to break it down into smaller segments. Earning 9 percent interest, if you deposit $59.77 a month for eight years, by the time your ten-year-old enters college, you will have enough saved for that first year.

How much do you have available for your special goals? $_____

Step Three is to allocate specific amounts to each goal. Larry and Diane decided that if they would allocate $151.17 per month in their savings account, they would have $6,000 in three years for their down payment. Looking at your goals, how much will you need to accomplish your goals within your time frame?

The first time you allocate resources to each goal you will discover that you have allocated more money than you have available. That is easy to do. That happens to me each time I have done this step. The solution is to go back over your plan and rearrange your allocation. Some goals may take longer to achieve. Some goals may only get $25 a month, this year. Each year, as your income increases, as other goals are reached, or as you decrease spending, you will be able to allocate more toward specific goals.

Step Four is to implement your plan. Make it work! Add your "special objectives" to your spending plan. Work with your spending plan for three months. Are you able to accomplish what you set out to do? Are there adjustments that need to be made?

Evaluate your plan on a regular basis. At least once a year check your

113

plan. Are you on schedule? Have you accomplished some goals? If so, celebrate! Each time you get a raise, bonus, or tax refund, apply that to your goals. As goals are reached, apply the money that went to those goals to other goals. Soon you will be celebrating your success.

Congratulations, you have a financial plan. It was not impossible, was it? You thought a financial plan was beyond your comprehension. You have discovered that financial planning is not knowledge to store in your mind but a way of life. It is not an ultimate destination on life's journey or a specific way of life. It is a never-ending journey that invites you to vision a future full of possibility and hope. From that future full of possibility and hope, it calls to you to take specific steps toward the realization of that vision.

Christian financial planning invites you to look beyond the accumulation and the action. It paints a picture of God and you together on an important mission. This is not money management. This is not about getting more. It is not even about money. It is about a journey and a partner traveling with you on that journey.

You are embarking on an exciting new journey with your financial plan. What you have developed is a plan for living—a life plan. The more you involve God as you travel through your life plan, the more satisfying it will be. Congratulations, and good luck!

APPENDIX A
SELECTED READING LIST

Chapter One
Hall, Douglas John. *Imaging God*. Eerdmans, 1986.
Haughey, John C. *The Holy Use of Money*. Doubleday, 1986.

Chapter Two
Felton-Collins, Victoria. *Couples and Money*. Bantam Books, 1990.
Foster, Richard. *Freedom of Simplicity*. Harper and Row, 1981.
Lindgren, Henry Clay. *Great Expectations: The Psychology of Money*. Kaufman, 1980.

Chapter Six
King, Frank. *In Time of Need: A Planning Workbook to Help Families, Friends, & Loved Ones to Prepare for Living and Dying*. Abingdon, 1985.

Chapter Seven
Moore, Gary D. *The Thoughtful Christian's Guide to Investing*. Zondervan Books, 1990.
Shames, Lawrence. *The Hunger for More: Searching for Values in an Age of Greed*. Time Books, 1989.
Stein, Benjamin. *Financial Passages*. Doubleday, 1985.

SAMPLE FORMS

Form 1:
Our Cash Flow

_____

(Date)

Income

Income One	Partnership Income
Income Two	Business Income
Income Three	Gifts
Interest and Dividend	Bonus
Rental Income	Other
Pension Income	
Social Security Income	
	Total Income

Fixed Expenses

Tithe	Installment Debt
Savings	Auto 1
Mortgage/Rent	Auto 2
Insurance Life—1	School
Life—2	Other
Auto	Allowance 1
Health	2
Disability	Children's Allowance
Home	1
	2

Special Objectives Expenses

Reduction of Debt	Vacation Fund
Credit Cards	Christmas Fund
School Loan	Children's Education
Installment	Retirement

Variable Expenses

Food	Doctor
Clothing	Dentist
Utilities	Transportation
Electrical	Entertainment
Gas	Gifts
Water	Household Supplies
Telephone	Miscellaneous

Total Expenses

_____

Our Net Worth

_____

(Date)

Assets

Cash & Cash Equivalents
    Checking
    Savings
    Money Market Funds
        Total Cash & Cash Equivalents   _____

Invested Assets

Certificates of Deposit	Pension (amount vested)
Other Bank Accounts	Money Owed You
Investment Accounts	IRA Accounts
Investment Property	Miscellaneous Invested Assets
Life Insurance (cash value)	

        Total Invested Assets   _____

Use Assets

House	Personal Property
Second Home	Household Furnishings
Autos	Personal Items
Boat	Miscellaneous Use Assets

        Total Use Assets   _____

        Total Assets
        Cash & Cash Equivalents   _____
        Invested Assets   _____
        Use Assets   _____

        Total Assets   _____

Liabilities (what you owe)

Mortgage Balance	Personal Loans
Auto Loan Balance	Bills Not Paid
Credit Card Balance	Miscellaneous Debts

        Total Liabilities   _____

Summary

Total Assets   _____
Minus Total Liabilities   _____

Total Net Worth   _____

Form 3:
Our Spending Plan
Jan.-June

Income	Annual Budget	January Budget	January Spent	February Budget	February Spent	March Budget	March Spent	April Budget	April Spent	May Budget	May Spent	June Budget	June Spent
Income One													
Income Two													
Income Three													
Interest and Dividend													
Rental Income													
Pension Income													
Social Security Income													
Partnership Income													
Business Income													
Gifts													
Bonus													
Other													
Total Income													

Our Spending Plan
July-Dec.

Income	July		August		September		October		November		December		Annual	
	Budget	Spent	Budget	Spent	Budget	Spent	Budget	Spent	Budget	Spent	Budget	Spent	Budget	Spent
Income One														
Income Two														
Income Three														
Interest and Dividend														
Rental Income														
Pension Income														
Social Security Income														
Partnership Income														
Business Income														
Gifts														
Bonus														
Other														
Total Income														

119

Our Spending Plan
Jan.-June

Fixed Expenses	Annual Budget	January Budget	January Spent	February Budget	February Spent	March Budget	March Spent	April Budget	April Spent	May Budget	May Spent	June Budget	June Spent
Tithe													
Savings													
Mortgage/Rent													
Insurance Life—1													
Life—2													
Auto													
Health													
Disability													
Home													
Installment Debt													
Auto 1													
Auto 2													
School													
Other													
Allowance 1													
2													
Children's Allowance													
2													
Total Fixed Expenses													

120

Our Spending Plan
July-Dec.

Fixed Expenses	July		August		September		October		November		December		Annual	
	Budget	Spent	Budget	Spent	Budget	Spent	Budget	Spent	Budget	Spent	Budget	Spent	Budget	Spent
Tithe														
Savings														
Mortgage/Rent														
Insurance Life—1														
Life—2														
Auto														
Health														
Disability														
Home														
Installment Debt														
Auto 1														
Auto 2														
School														
Other														
Allowance 1														
2														
Children's Allowance														
2														
Total Fixed Expenses														

Our Spending Plan
Jan.-June

This Year's Special Objectives	Annual Budget	January Budget	January Spent	February Budget	February Spent	March Budget	March Spent	April Budget	April Spent	May Budget	May Spent	June Budget	June Spent
Reduction of Debt													
Credit Cards													
School Loan													
Installment													
Vacation Fund													
Christmas Fund													
Children's Education													
Retirement													
Total Special Objectives													

Our Spending Plan
July-Dec.

This Year's Special Objectives	July		August		September		October		November		December		Annual	
	Budget	Spent	Budget	Spent	Budget	Spent	Budget	Spent	Budget	Spent	Budget	Spent	Budget	Spent
Reduction of Debt														
Credit Cards														
School Loan														
Installment														
Vacation Fund														
Christmas Fund														
Children's Education														
Retirement														
Total Special Objectives														

Our Spending Plan
Jan.-June

Variable Expenses	Annual Budget	January Budget	January Spent	February Budget	February Spent	March Budget	March Spent	April Budget	April Spent	May Budget	May Spent	June Budget	June Spent
Food													
Clothing													
Utilities													
Electrical													
Gas													
Water													
Telephone													
Doctor													
Dentist													
Transportation													
Entertainment													
Gifts													
Household supplies													
Taxes—Local & State													
Federal													
Social Security													
Emergencies													
Miscellaneous													
Total Variable Expenses													

Our Spending Plan
July-Dec.

Variable Expenses	July Budget	July Spent	August Budget	August Spent	September Budget	September Spent	October Budget	October Spent	November Budget	November Spent	December Budget	December Spent	Annual Budget	Annual Spent
Food														
Clothing														
Utilities														
Electrical														
Gas														
Water														
Telephone														
Doctor														
Dentist														
Transportation														
Entertainment														
Gifts														
Household supplies														
Taxes—Local & State														
Federal														
Social Security														
Emergencies														
Miscellaneous														
Total Variable Expenses														

Our Spending Plan
Jan.-June

Summary	Annual Budget	January	February	March	April	May	June
Total Income							
Expenses							
Fixed Expenses							
Special Objectives							
Variable Expenses							
Total Expenses							
Difference							

Our Spending Plan
July-Dec.

Summary	July	August	September	October	November	December	Annual Totals
Total Income							
Expenses							
Fixed Expenses							
Special Objectives							
Variable Expenses							
Total Expenses							
Difference							

Appendix C

IDEAS FOR GROUP STUDIES

Jerry and Patti were thrilled by their emerging financial freedom. "You know," Jerry reflected, "we could never have done this alone." It is not just the skills a third party brings to a financial planning process, but an accountability to another person or thing (a class) beyond ourselves that helps us do what we know we need to do.

Christians and Money was written for the individual Christian. At the same time, the possibility of small group discussions, using the book, can be helpful. There is a difference between reading a resource and using it as a guide for small group response. Using this resource as a small group study will open up the opportunity for individuals to share something very personal. Sharing personal financial information, however, may be threatening. We suggest, therefore, that leaders use hypothetical situations, or fictitious case studies, instead of personal sharing.

Use this book to guide groups in discussion in the following 3 models:

Model 1: *Three Sessions* (2 hours each)

Each participant will read *Christians and Money* prior to each session. Sessions may be each evening for a week, or over a three-week period.

Session
1. Christians and Money: A Faithful Partnership—Guest leader: Pastor
   Developing a Money Sense—Guest leader: Psychologist
2. Managing for Financial Freedom—Guest leader: Financial Planner
   Dealing with Debt—Guest leader: Credit Counselor
3. Estate Planning and the Christian—Guest leaders: Estate Planning Attorney,
   Development Director

Model 2: *Six-Week Class* (1 hour each)

Each participant will read *Christians and Money* prior to each session.

Week
1. The Christian and Money—A Faithful Partnership
2. Developing a Christian Money Sense
3. Managing for Financial Freedom
4. Dealing with Debt
5. Estate Planning and the Christian
6. Life Planning

Model 3: *Thirteen-Week Class* (1 hour each)

Each participant will read *Christians and Money* prior to each session.

Week
1. The Christian and Money—A Faithful Partnership
2. The Steward: A Biblical Symbol Come of Age
3. Developing a Christian Money Sense
4. Guest Leader: Psychologist
5. Managing for Financial Freedom
6. Guest Leader: Financial Planner
7. Designing a Plan for Spending
8. Dealing with Debt
9. Guest Leader: Credit Counselor
10. Estate Planning and the Christian
11. Guest Leader: Estate Planning Attorney on Wills
12. Guest Leader: Estate Planning Attorney (continued)
13. Life Planning

If you are considering this study for a small group using any of these models, you can receive additional help by contacting: Section on Stewardship, General Board of Discipleship, P.O. Box 840, Nashville, TN 37202-0840.

128